Rebels with Insufficient Cause

Rebels with Insufficient Cause

Americans of African Descent, the Victim Mentality,
and Value Formation through the Family

By
J. M. SPARROW

WIPF & STOCK · Eugene, Oregon

REBELS WITH INSUFFICIENT CAUSE
Americans of African Descent, the Victim Mentality, and Value Formation through
the Family

Wipf & Stock
An Imprint of Wipf and Stock Publishers
199 W. 8th Ave., Suite 3
Eugene, OR 97401

www.wipfandstock.com

PAPERBACK ISBN: 978-1-5326-5293-6
HARDCOVER ISBN: 978-1-5326-5294-3
EBOOK ISBN: 978-1-5326-5295-0

Manufactured in the U.S.A.   09/26/18

To Josiah, my son,

and Micah, my daughter,

may our Heavenly Father,

through our Lord Jesus Christ

grant you grace to complete the race,

and finish it well

Contents

Abstract | ix

Preface | xi

Chapter 1
Why the Big Fuss? | 1

Chapter 2
Self-Perceptions | 17

Chapter 3
The Shared Human Experience | 38

Chapter 4
A New Value System: Biblical Family Formation | 60

Chapter 5
Practical Helps | 84

Bibliography | 103

Abstract

Why have Americans of African descent, as a group, not progressed as much as other racial groups in the areas of economics, education, traditional family development, and socialization? There seem to be two extremes in answer to this question. The liberal side seems to blame the system. The reason many black Americans fall behind other groups is blamed on institutional racism or something ingrained in the American system that curtail flourishing for Americans of African descent. On the other hand, most on the moderate and conservative sides do not deny the black experience through slavery and Jim Crow. Yet, they emphasize that Americans of African descent can do better by practicing the same tried and true methods that made other Americans successful.

This book will argue the point that the major source of the problems in the black community has its origin in the demise of the traditional family. Statistics, written testimony, historical fact, common sense, and a biblical Christian worldview will be used to help pinpoint and offer solutions to the problem. The family that is founded on one mother and one father who are married to each other and who respond to one another as well as their children, in the way the Bible prescribes, is the only normal family. Anything else can only be second best. When children are socialized in a loving and disciplined environment, they have the greatest probability to flourish as human beings.

Preface

In 1958, then Senator John F. Kennedy wrote a book entitled *A Nation of Immigrants* in which he described all Americans as immigrants or descendants of immigrants, "except for one group."[1] If each immigrant group is to be successful in this present economy, it is important for the group to assimilate into the dominant culture, at least to some extent. This certainly does not mean that ethnic groups must lose their cultural distinctiveness; but it does mean that they must submit to the standards of business, culture, and language or those very distinctive qualities that all Americans share. Many Americans of African descent have resisted this assimilation and, as a result, set themselves against those American distinctive qualities. Furthermore, many of them have embraced a self-perception of victimization. As well, due to the modern view of what it means to be a black person, some have turned to lives of opposition against the dominant culture to embrace aberrancy, refusing to value the very principles that made America great like religiosity, family, education, and a strong work ethic.

Although they may not be migrants in the normal sense because of the history of American slavery, Americans of African descent must accept new perceptions of themselves if they are to do better as a people group. Every successful group of migrants had to submit to certain basic norms in accordance with the dominant culture. An increasing number of Americans of African descent are doing well and making good progress financially and socially, but too many remain a part of the underclass. Therefore, if Americans of African descent, as a group, are to better assimilate into society, they must reject the victim mentality that prevents them from attaining a higher social status, accept primary responsibility for their own successes or failures, and support value formation through the biblical concept of family.

1. Kennedy, *Nation of Immigrants*, 2.

The term "Americans of African descent" will be used for black Americans rather than the term "African American" in this work. Americans of African descent must recognize that they are "Americans" above being "African" in order to be successful in this economy.[2] The first generations out of Africa who came or were brought to the United States were more African than American, but contemporary black Americans have since formed their own culture and norms. They should not be viewed as second-class Americans; this country belongs as much to them as it does any other citizen group. When black Americans realize this, they must join hands with all other Americans and embrace the value system that made America great. Resisting standard English, dressing in hip hop garb with sagging pants, and acting like a thug does not make a person black. A person is black because he or she was born that way. Americans of African descent need to discard these contemporary views of blackness and embrace others that can bring success to themselves as well as their children.

As well, the term "black" will also be used because of its ubiquitous usage in opposition to "white," "Hispanic," and "Asian." Although Hispanic people may be considered white or black under certain conditions, the term "Hispanic" will be used in this paper of all primarily Spanish-speaking ethnicities.

The term "Americans of European descent," "Americans of Spanish-speaking countries descent," or "Americans of Asian descent" will not be used in this book. Black people are more widely known as African American than white people as European American or Hispanic people as Hispanic American, although those designations would not be wrong. The point is that America is made up of various kinds of races, so once a person of any ethnicity becomes an American citizen, he or she should see himself or herself as an American first, and each citizen's loyalty should be to his or her country, America, and not to their place of origin or to some subgroup. Only then can each group feel comfortable to join in with those values and enterprises that make a person distinctly American, rather than seeing himself or herself as an outsider. Americans of African descent were once made to feel like outsiders due to slavery and Jim Crow laws. However, although prejudice still exists within the hearts of sinful human beings of all races and against all races, there is no reason for Americans of African descent to remain outsiders today, except by their own actions.

---

2. McWhorter, *Winning the Race*, 46–47.

The victim mentality will be addressed here. "Victimology" is defined as a mindset of a person or group that adopts being a victim as a way to his, her, or their struggles and distinctiveness. Quite often, victimhood among Americans of African descent is exaggerated and used as an excuse for failure to thrive under certain circumstances.[3] There are times when people are actual victims and that should not be minimized. It is a well-known fact that Africans were brought to the United States, as well as other countries, to be slaves. These people were victims. They were robbed of their families, their cultures, their homeland, and their basic rights as humans. After being freed from slavery, the rights given to other citizens were denied to them. They were still victims. Today, those shameful impediments to human freedom have been eradicated. Although prejudice still exists in the hearts of sinful humans, there no longer remain any barriers to any American, including black Americans, which can legally keep them from accomplishing the American ideal. Considering that Americans of African descent serve in the highest political and social offices in America and are found in every major profession ubiquitously, they can no longer blame the system of institutional racism on their failure to keep up with other racial groups. It will be proven in this work that many Americans of African descent are victims of their own making.

Finally, value formation through the traditional family will be emphasized in this book. The traditional family will be defined by a biblical understanding of how God made the family in the beginning. Jesus affirmed that when God created humans, "he who created them from the beginning made them male and female," and then made the proclamation, "What therefore God has joined together let not man separate."[4] Thus the foundation of the ideal family unit is one that contains a woman and a man joined together in a lifelong covenant of unity to "be fruitful and multiply" or procreate and mentor offspring for the betterment of society.[5]

In the West, the secularization of society has affected the whole of life. The values a person holds dear, the basis of education, political ideologies, views of marriage, legislation, as well as arts like music, theatre, and other aspects of popular culture have all been affected by the public silencing of

---

3. McWhorter, *Losing the Race*, 169.

4. Matthew 19:4, 6. All biblical quotations will be made from the English Standard Version of the Bible unless otherwise stated.

5. Genesis 1:28.

Christianity.[6] Thus, one's religious views, if they are actually practiced, will affect one's family life.[7] Just about every study shows that children are better off when they are raised by their biological mother and father.[8]

The traditional family unit is rare in households of Americans of African descent and becoming rarer in other American households.[9] If Americans of African descent are going to slow the decline in areas of economics and education, and promote values that will deter crime and aberrant behavior (sociological factors), they are going to have to rediscover the value of getting married according to biblical standards, remaining married, and raising their biological children together. Anything that is substituted for the traditional unit will never be good enough. God made an orderly world and gave humans rules by which to live. Those rules were made for humanity's good, like parameters in which humans should live.[10] When those rules are violated, God's orderly creation turns a chaotic mess. Americans who are black are experiencing that chaos today at a greater level than other ethnic groups. May God Almighty grant Americans of African descent, as well as all human beings, grace and strength to discern and correct self-destructive behavior and walk the path the Creator marked out for humans to go.

I want to give special thanks to my academic advisor, Dr. Evan Lenow, who, without his help, I would have had a much more difficult time completing this work. I also want to thank my loving wife, Carla. Without her support, I would be far less of a man.

6. Eberstadt, *How the West Really Lost God*, 7.

7. Eberstadt, *How the West Really Lost God*, 93.

8. Gennetian, "One or Two Parents? Half or Step Siblings? The effect of Family Structure on Young Children's Achievement," 418.

9. Banks, *Is Marriage for White People?*, 6–8.

10. Deuteronomy 10:12–13.

Chapter 1

Why the Big Fuss?

Cornel West began his book, *Race Matters*, by saying, "Black people in the United States differ from all other modern people owing to the unprecedented levels of unregulated and unrestrained violence directed at them."[1] Yes, there have been injustices directed toward Americans of African descent in America. Yes, growing up in most black households, even today, is different than growing up in most white ones. However, are the conditions in which many Americans of African descent live today due to "the unprecedented levels of unregulated and unrestrained violence directed at them," or could it be due to other causes? West assumes, as others, that just because black people do not show equal results in the areas of economics, education, criminology, and other forms of culture that there must be continued and institutional discrimination against Americans of African descent.[2] However, this may not always be the case. Although the statistics are real, one cannot assume that unequal outcomes in these areas today are always due to discrimination. There may be other factors at work. This chapter will discuss the dilemma, the major intellectual thoughts about the causes of that dilemma, and the best solutions based on the available evidence.

---

1. West, *Race Matters*, xiii.
2. West, *Race Matters*, xiv.

The Dilemma

Why the big fuss about Americans of African descent? Why single them out above all other major racial groups in America? It is because Americans of African descent, as a group, suffer more in the areas of economics, education, traditional family development, and socialization than any other American racial group. While there are always individual exceptions to the rule, Americans of African descent fall behind other major racial groups (white, Hispanic, and Asian) in just about all these areas.

First, Americans of African descent have the lowest median income of all major racial groups. While the median household income for Asians was slightly higher than whites in 2011, Hispanics and blacks followed whites at approximately 68 percent and 59 percent of white homes, respectively.[3] Furthermore, three times the amount of black Americans live in poverty per capita as whites and are 29 percent less likely to own a home.[4] The largest economic disparity seems to be in the area of wealth. Wealth is determined by "assets minus liabilities in Census Bureau data," or in other words, wealth is defined by how much a family is worth if they liquidate all their assets and turn them into cash.[5] Although the wealth maintained by Asian and white families is about the same, white households had thirteen times the wealth of black households.[6] Hispanic families' wealth is slightly higher than black households.[7]

As well, Americans of African descent fall behind other major racial groups, with the exception of Hispanics, in the area of education. Although high school graduation rates were essentially the same for whites, Asians, and blacks in 2012 with 92 percent, 89 percent, and 86 percent respectively, Hispanics lagged behind with only a 65 percent graduation rate.[8] However, when the college completion rate is observed for 2012, 51 percent of Asians

3. "Chapter 3: Demographic and Economic Data, by Race" The median incomes of the various major racial groups in 2011 were $68,521 for Asians, $67,175 for whites, $40,007 for Hispanics, and $39,760 for blacks.

4. "Chapter 3: Demographic and Economic Data, by Race." In 2012, 73 percent of whites owned a home, compared to 57 percent of Asians, 46 percent of Hispanics, and only 44 percent of blacks.

5. "Chapter 3: Demographic and Economic Data, by Race."

6. Drake, "5 Facts about Race in America."

7. "Chapter 3: Demographic and Economic Data, by Race." Hispanic households' net wealth was $7,843 in 2011 while black families' net wealth was $6,446.

8. "Chapter 3: Demographic and Economic Data, by Race."

completed college while 34 percent of whites, 21 percent of blacks, and 15 percent of Hispanics finished with their baccalaureate degrees.[9]

Furthermore, Americans of African descent struggle more than other racial groups in the area of marriage and family. Some Americans of African descent are just not getting married. One survey showed that "three out of ten black non-Hispanics born during 1957–1964 did not marry by age 46, while the same statistic for whites remained close to 1 in 10."[10] Although marriage is declining in all major racial groups, Americans of African descent suffer the most. In 1960, the marriage rates between whites, Hispanics, and blacks were fairly close. At that time, 74 percent of white adults were married as were 72 percent of Hispanics and 61 percent of blacks. However, by 2011, the rate had fallen to 55 percent of whites, 47 percent of Hispanics, and only 31 percent of black adults were married. As well, Americans of African descent lead in the category of out-of-wedlock births with 72 percent of all births to unmarried couples. The Hispanic out-of-wedlock birth rate follows with 53 percent, and the white out-of-wedlock birth rate was 29 percent in 2011.[11]

Another startling statistic is the incarceration rate of black males. Of all the inmates incarcerated in the United States, blacks, who make up about 13.3 percent of the total population,[12] account for 37.6 percent of all incarcerations[13] and are "seven times more likely than whites to have a prison record."[14] The incarceration statistic is a devastating one to Americans of African descent because having a prison record greatly diminishes sociological and economic ascendancy. It is often claimed that the system is unjustly biased against black males, yet the greatest propagators of violent crime are young black males. According to the Federal Bureau of Investigation's Uniform Crime Report data for 2013, close to 44 percent of all murders were committed by Americans of African descent, and the far greatest majority of those murders were committed by males.[15] The greatest age concentration of those who committed those crimes was between twenty

9. "Chapter 3: Demographic and Economic Data, by Race."
10. Aughinbaugh, Robles, and Sun, "Marriage and Divorce."
11. "Chapter 3: Demographic and Economic Data, by Race."
12. "Quick Facts United States."
13. "Inmate Race," Federal Bureau of Prisons.
14. Western and Wildeman, "Black Family and Mass Incarceration," 232.
15. "Expanded Homicide Data Table 6."

and thirty.[16] Viewed in conjunction with all the other statistics presented, these are mostly black men who were raised fatherless, did not do well in school, and forged their way through troubled pasts. In his book, *Bringing Up Boys*, James Dobson spoke of a greeting-card company that gave free cards to inmates in a federal prison to send to their mothers on Mother's Day. The response was so overwhelming that the company had to bring in more cards. However, when they did the same for Father's Day, no prisoner responded.[17] This event speaks loudly in reference to the correlation between aberrant behavior and fatherlessness.

It is a well-known fact that married couples do better in all the above categories. Married people are more likely to be in the upper income bracket and enjoy higher educational achievements than unmarried adults, while 53 percent of unmarried females with at least one child live in the lower income bracket.[18] During the 1960s, the marriage rates between those who finished college and those who did not were comparable. However, those who finish college today marry at a higher rate than those who do not.[19] The late Charles Colson quoted in his book *A Dance with Deception* a *Reader's Digest* opinion poll that showed a deep divide between the cultural values of voters with children and those who had none. A greater number of voters with children were against abortion, supported mothers staying home with children, and were against gay marriage. Colson concluded, "It seems that the experience of parenthood itself deepens and matures young adults. The responsibility, the sacrifice, the commitment, and the new sense of the future all combine to shape parents' attitudes on key moral issues."[20] In his book *Coming Apart: the State of White America, 1960–2010* Charles Murray introduced four factors: industriousness, honesty, marriage, and religiosity, which he referred to as "founding virtues," or those deeply-held beliefs that define what made America great.[21] Murray further said that before 1960, when no-fault divorce did not exist, speedy divorces were only possible in Nevada, and divorce in many states was only granted on the basis of either adultery or cruelty.[22] The 1960s mark the time when many

16. "Table 311. Murder Victims by Age, Sex, and Race: 2008."
17. Dobson, *Bringing Up Boys*, 60.
18. "Changes in Income Status Vary Across Demographic Groups."
19. "Chapter 3: Demographic and Economic Data, by Race."
20. Charles Colson, *Dance with Deception*, 151–52.
21. Charles Murray, *Coming Apart*, 130.
22. Charles Murray, *Coming Apart*, 150.

sociologists agree that America made a turn toward a more liberal society,[23] or as Murray put it, society made a "cultural transformation."[24] Views toward marriage seemed to change at that point as well, and these changes seemed to affect Americans of African descent more severely than other racial groups. Bruce Western and Christopher Wildeman have shown that marriage itself is a major deterrent and rehabilitator of criminal behavior in black males. Marriage provides responsibility, close positive familial bonds, and separates black males from other young men who are involved in aberrant behavior.[25]

Various Answers to the Dilemma in Question

As the prior section confirms, Americans of African descent, as a group, face huge difficulties and seem to fall toward the bottom of economic development, educational achievement, traditional family development, and societal socialization. The question is not whether the community is affected by these issues; it is affected so much that many today still feel that Americans of African descent should be given a handicap, so to speak, or should be judged by a different standard than the remainder of society in the form of affirmative action. Although affirmative action was necessary and useful during the 1960s and 1970s because of former law-based discrimination, Americans of African descent should be offended today when it is supposed that they need preferential treatment above all others because they cannot measure up. Should black applicants, for example, be accepted into colleges and universities with lower SAT scores than other races, just because they are black?[26] The debate continues. The major source of disagreement in the intellectual community seems to lie in the causes of these pathologies; hence, various solutions are offered depending on what the cause is perceived to be. In essence, the liberal side contends that since America is the major contributor to black community problems through slavery and discrimination, government programs and the like should be offered as the solution. However, those on the moderate and conservative sides propose that government programs should only be temporary, a stepping-stone to help people get out of tough times. Nonetheless, the

23. Eberstadt, *How the West Really Lost God*, 131.

24. Murray, *Coming Apart*, 1.

25. Western and Wildeman, "Black Family and Mass Incarceration," 233–34.

26. McWhorter, *Losing the Race*, 169.

true onus rests on the personal responsibility of individuals, families, and communities. What is the best answer?

In 1965, Daniel P. Moynihan wrote *The Negro Family: The Case for National Action*.[27] In this groundbreaking report, Moynihan did not overlook the setbacks blacks encountered due to slavery and discrimination.[28] Yet he still affirmed that the major cause of the dilemmas among lower-class blacks is the breakdown of the family and added proof by reporting that the illegitimacy rate among blacks went from 16.8 percent in 1940 to 23.6 percent at the time of that writing, a figure that is dwarfed in comparison to what it is today.[29] Moynihan has been widely criticized for oversimplifying the issue, but time has seemed to offer authentication for his findings. The stated objective of the Moynihan report was to manifest the growing problem in the black community; it was not so much to offer solutions.[30] However, this work was pivotal in getting the conversation started about what can be done to strengthen the black community, especially during the time following the passing of the Civil Rights Act of 1964.

Another pivotal work that resurrected the conversation was *Come on People: On the Path from Victims to Victors,* written in 2007 by Bill Cosby and Alvin Poussaint.[31] This work was a follow-up of Cosby's 2004 diatribe at the NAACP fiftieth anniversary commemoration of *Brown v. the Board of Education.* Cosby and Poussaint stressed that blacks should accept personal responsibility and stop blaming others or, in other words, they should stop playing the victim.[32] Cosby and Poussaint offer good secular values and practical wisdom. The reason this book is so substantial to the conversation is because, as Craig Mitchell reported, "Until Cosby gave his speech at Constitution Hall, these feelings were rarely aired in public."[33] So, regardless of Cosby's personal problems of late, the book is still relevant to the conversation.[34]

27. Moynihan, *Negro Family.*

28. Moynihan, *Negro Family,* 15, 47.

29. Moynihan, *Negro Family,* 5, 7. As mentioned earlier in this book, the out-of-wedlock birth rate among blacks is presently 72 percent.

30. Moynihan, *Negro Family,* 47.

31. Cosby and Poussaint, *Come on People.*

32. Moynihan, *Negro Family,* 39–40.

33. Mitchell, "Rev. Michael Eric Dyson: An Analysis," 201.

34. Tenfani, Serrano, and Goffard, "Sex-Crime Charge Marks a Turning Point in the Bill Cosby Saga."

One of the most influential books written in response to Cosby's speech was Michael Eric Dyson's *Is Bill Cosby Right?: Or Has the Black Middle Class Lost Its Mind?*[35] Although Dyson's book predated Cosby and Poussaint's book and was written in response to Cosby's 2004 speech, it still presents a clear opposition to Cosby and Poussaint's thoughts. Dyson accused Cosby of being "ill-informed" and that his speech "reinforce(s) suspicions about black humanity."[36] As Craig Mitchell said, Dyson's book was mainly a personal attack against Cosby and those who share his thinking.[37] Dyson feels that Cosby "let many of these whites off the hook" because the major source of pathology in the black community is "structural features" rather than an "overemphasis of personal responsibility."[38] In other words, the sources of the problems in the black community are whites and the structures they put in place. In chapter 4 of *Is Bill Cosby Right?*, titled "Family Values," Dyson spends much of the chapter blasting Cosby about the shortcomings in his own family and accusing Cosby for wrongfully vilifying the poor.[39] Nonetheless, rather than offer solutions for some of the obvious problems that Americans of African descent face, he praises "gangstas," those who through their "lifestyle and ideology of the outlaw, the rebel, and the bandit challenge the corrupt norms of the state, the government, and the rule of law in society," and "gayz," or "the aggressively, progressively gay, lesbian, bisexual, transgender presence in black America."[40] Although Dyson is an ordained Baptist minister, or one who is supposed to interpret God's word to humanity, the question about how God may see these matters never arises.[41]

Others, like Cornel West, also believe that the perils Americans of African descent face should not be sought primarily in personal responsibility of the individual but in the American structures of capitalism and oppression of blacks. West contends that any "serious discussion" about racial issues should not spring from problems in the black community but from defects in the American system.[42] While West claims not to absolve indi-

35. Dyson, *Is Bill Cosby Right?*

36. Dyson, *Is Bill Cosby Right?*, 2.

37. Mitchell, "Rev. Michael Eric Dyson," 201–3.

38. Dyson, *Is Bill Cosby Right?*, 5.

39. Dyson, *Is Bill Cosby Right?*, 141–66, 172.

40. Dyson, *Is Bill Cosby Right?*, 174–75.

41. Mitchell, "Rev. Michael Eric Dyson," 197.

42. West, *Race Matters*, 6.

vidual blacks of aberrant behavior, he blames their conduct on a response to capitalism or "a jungle ruled by a cutthroat market" where blacks lack needed resources.[43] However, as shown above, most other races are thriving in this capitalistic society. As a matter of fact, the most prosperous countries on Earth are capitalistic countries.[44] Why are things different for Americans of African descent? Is West inferring that blacks are inherently weaker than those races that are thriving? The very fact of their continued existence shows that Americans of African descent are a strong people.

Tavis Smiley, on the other hand, seeks to make the black community stronger by keeping one's blackness in the forefront and by advocating a type of social segregation from whites. In his "Ten Challenges to Black America," Smiley encourages Americans of African descent to spend money at black-owned businesses and seek black employees at those businesses.[45] While Smiley agrees with other liberals that America is a debtor to Americans of African descent, he feels the black community's emphasis should be on boosting itself. "Self-determination, self-reliance, and self-respect" should be the black man's or woman's focus rather than "looking to white America for recognition and acceptance."[46] Thus, Americans of African descent should not care how they appear to other Americans. They should do all they can to boost themselves and their communities. While Smiley's emphasis on doing better for oneself and one's community is commendable, Americans of African descent cannot truly be successful unless they are willing to recognize that they are part of the larger community of American citizens. The larger business culture in America is not just white culture; it belongs to every American citizen.[47] As well, Smiley failed to address glaring issues such as black-on-black crime, out-of-wedlock pregnancies, and the anti-educational bias that is plaguing black communities across the United States.

In opposition to liberal thinkers, black intellectuals on the conservative and moderate sides seem to agree with the basic premises of Moynihan, Cosby, and Poussaint. Anthony Bradley contested that the pernicious behaviors brought to light in *Come on People* like "the black male crisis, out-of-wedlock births, the breakdown of the family and community, bad

43. West, *Race Matters*, 25.

44. Ferguson, *Great Degeneration*, 21–25.

45. Smiley, "Ten Challenges to Black America," 5.

46. Smiley, "Ten Challenges to Black America," 10–11.

47. McWhorter, *Losing the Race*, 51.

parenting, substandard education, media consumption without discernment, poor health choices, violence, and poverty," manifest the consequences of the fall of humanity into sin.[48] Juan Williams warned about the message underlying the ideas of liberal black leaders that purport that white America controls the issues that plague Americans of African descent today. The message is, "Whites have all the power, you are weak, you can't make a difference for yourself or your family, and you will always be the victim."[49] Williams further proposed that the reason why Cosby and others brought attention to these issues was to encourage Americans of African descent to take advantage of "the amazing opportunities" afforded to them through the Civil Rights struggles.[50]

John McWhorter highlighted four problems the victim mentality produces.[51] First, the victim mentality puts forward the idea that Americans of African descent are not good enough. It seems to give "failure, lack of effort, and criminology a tacit stamp of approval."[52] When an American of African descent is chosen to a high ranking or important position, do people question whether the person is really qualified, or was the appointment a product of affirmative action? Does the person who was placed in the position or job question himself or herself about whether he or she is truly qualified? Second, victimology inhibits a can-do attitude by focusing on the difficulties one may face. It emphasizes negativity. Other racial groups also face difficulties, but they do not use them as an excuse not to thrive. Third, the victim mentality highlights and enlivens racism. By bringing attention to perceived prejudice and discrimination that sometimes does not exist, a consciousness of race is always up front. McWhorter debunked as a myth the popular conviction held by many Americans of African descent that racism in America is substantially the same today as it was before the Civil Rights movement.[53] The fact that Barack Obama became the first black president of the United States and was elected to two terms should give added support to McWhorter's assertions. Finally, the victim mentality insults the memory of those who risked their lives and freedom to secure civil

48. Bradley, "Redeemed and Healed for Mission," 139.
49. Williams, *Enough*, 69.
50. Williams, *Enough*, 68.
51. McWhorter, *Losing the Race*, 43–49.
52. McWhorter, *Losing the Race*, 43.
53. McWhorter, *Losing the Race*, 6–8.

rights for all races. All those men and women wanted was an equal chance; they did not want preferential treatment.

There is a clear demarcation between liberals and moderates/conservatives on where the burden of responsibility should lie. Should it lie with the sins of American society or should Americans of African descent themselves take the blame? It seems that the liberal side constructed a straw man. Few, if any, moderate or conservative thinkers deny the effects of slavery and Jim Crow on the present conditions of Americans of African descent. However, they assert that if true progress is to be made, individuals, families, and communities must take responsibility for their own lives.

What Early Black Leaders Wanted

What did the early American of African descent leadership believe and hold dear? What did they desire for black Americans? Three of the most influential leaders will be examined: Booker T. Washington, W. E. B. Dubois, and Frederick Douglass. They were fully aware that they had been victims. Two of the three had been slaves, but they all rejected the victim mentality. Although their ideologies did not totally line up, the only help requested by each of them was a level playing field so that Americans of African descent would be able to compete in a free society.

Booker T. Washington was born a slave on a Virginia farm in the mid- to late 1850s. Since he was a slave, he was unsure of the actual date.[54] After being freed by the Emancipation Proclamation, he founded Tuskegee Institute to teach Americans of African descent industry and agriculture, along with personal grooming and manners.[55] His philosophy is best known from his Atlanta Exposition Address, where he encouraged Americans of African descent to "cast down your buckets where you are."[56] In other words, he encouraged the black population to take advantage of what was offered to them at the time. Washington related that there was "as much dignity in the field as in writing a poem."[57] He also accepted segregation from whites by using the illustration, "In all things that are purely social we can be as separate as the fingers, yet one as the hand in all things essential to mutual

---

54. Washington, *Up from Slavery*, 1.

55. Washington, *Up from Slavery*, 126–27.

56. Washington, *Up from Slavery*, 218–25.

57. Washington, *Up from Slavery*, 220.

progress."[58] Many whites praised Washington for his speech and accepted his philosophy.[59] However, others felt that this speech and Washington's views on segregation precipitated the soon-following legislation that enacted Jim Crow (separate but equal) laws.[60] Thus, many were not so enthusiastic at this compromise.

W. E. B. Dubois was born in Great Barrington, Massachusetts, in 1868 and was never a slave. He was educated at Fisk and Harvard Universities as well as the University of Berlin.[61] Dubois distinguished himself as the first American of African descent to receive a PhD from Harvard and became a leading intellectual voice in early black studies. In his famous book *The Souls of Black Folk* he began his chapter "On Mr. Booker T. Washington and Others," with the words, "Easily the most striking thing in the history of the American Negro since 1876 is the ascendency of Mr. Booker T. Washington."[62] Hence, regardless of disagreement in philosophy, Dubois had great respect for Washington. However, he referred to Washington's Atlanta Exposition Address as the "Atlanta Compromise" because he saw that it was being interpreted by the larger society as a renunciation for any type of political equality between whites and blacks.[63] Dubois distinguished Washington's doctrine as one that "overlooked certain elements of true manhood" and was "too narrow."[64] Washington was willing to take advantage of what was given to his race by whites in American society, but Dubois wanted more; he wanted full equality with whites socially, educationally, and politically. Dubois accused Washington of representing the old slave "attitude of adjustment and submission" that "accepts the alleged inferiority of the Negro races."[65]

The third early Civil Rights leader that will be discussed is Frederick Douglass. Douglass was born a slave in 1818 in Maryland but escaped around age 20 and became one of the nation's leading black voices.[66] One of his most memorable speeches was titled "Self-Made Men" and was

58. Washington, *Up from Slavery*, 222.

59. Washington, *Up from Slavery*, 225–26.

60. Hare, "W. E. Burghardt Du Bois," xxi.

61. Poussaint, "Souls of Black Folk," xxviii–xi.

62. Dubois, *Souls of Black Folk*, 79.

63. Dubois, *Souls of Black Folk*, 80.

64. Dubois, *Souls of Black Folk*, 82.

65. Dubois, *Souls of Black Folk*, 87.

66. Daley, "Editor's Note," v.

delivered on April 6, 1894, at the Indian Industrial School in Carlisle, Pennsylvania.[67] Douglass neither asked anyone to give him a handicap nor did he ask for welfare. He said, "A man may, at times, get something for nothing, but it will, in his hands, amount to nothing."[68] He went further to explain the secret to success as "Work! Work!! Work!!! Work!!!!"[69] How did he want his fellow Americans of African descent to be treated after slavery? His answer was to "Give the Negro fair play and let him alone. . .It is not fair play to start the Negro out in life, from nothing and with nothing, while others start with the advantage of a thousand years behind them."[70] In other words, Douglass was not asking for a handout but a leg up. He used the illustration that blacks were expected in the past to make "bricks without straw; now give him straw. Give him all the facilities for honest and successful livelihood."[71] Douglass did not ask for reparations for all the years that Americans of African descent spent in slavery but related that "the nearest approach to justice for the Negro for the past is to do him justice in the present. . .If he fails, then let him fail."[72] Douglass continued by quoting Thackeray in saying that "All men are about as lazy as they can afford to be."[73] Hence, Douglass believed that it is the idea of necessity that will springboard Americans of African descent into doing what they must do to survive.

Douglass, Dubois, and Washington each advocated for hard work in the black community rather than handouts. They did not ask for anything other than an even playing field. Dubois and Washington did not agree on how to better the cause of Americans of African descent, but they both agreed that blacks would have to take the lead themselves to do better. Being the deep thinker he was, Dubois spoke about how American blacks were always made to feel a "twoness," in the sense of being both black and American. Because of their blackness, many people in Dubois's day were never truly accepted as American. His answer was neither to "Africanize America," nor for the black person to "bleach his Negro soul in a flood of white America," but to join the two so blacks can be "both a Negro and

67. Douglass, "Self-Made Men," 125.
68. Douglass, "Self-Made Men," 133.
69. Douglass, "Self-Made Men," 134.
70. Douglass, "Self-Made Men," 135.
71. Douglass, "Self-Made Men," 135.
72. Douglass, "Self-Made Men," 135.
73. Douglass, "Self-Made Men," 135.

an American, without being cursed and spit upon by his fellows, without having the doors of opportunity closed roughly in his face."[74] America has made greater strides toward that goal in today's society. However, many blacks are creating for themselves a new twoness, and it is drastically crippling many in the black community. Douglass said, "If you want to make your son helpless, you need not cripple him with bullet or bludgeon, but simply place him beyond the reach of necessity and surround him with ease and luxury."[75] This clearly shows where Douglass would stand today on the issues of reparations and welfare. He obviously believed that the necessity to do for oneself, as long as the opportunities are fair, is the motivation for success or failure. That is the spirit of capitalism.

Disparities, Discrimination, or Something Else?

Thomas Sowell deeply questioned certain presuppositions held by many intellectuals today in reference to race relations. From the educational realm to the American law courts, any type of disparity of results between groups or individuals is considered to be clear-cut proof of some type of discrimination.[76] Sowell argued that just because great discrepancies on issues such as intelligence quotients (IQ), income, and crime rates among races exist, intellectuals tend to blame these things on discrimination or sometimes even genes, with little or no empirical evidence.[77] Sowell went on to say that impediments to thrive do not always have to come from outside the group. Long-term cultural norms among groups can deter growth within that group.[78] Sowell concluded that even if there was proof that every person of each race began with some form of innate inequality, there are far too many variables that can affect intelligence, economics, and other factors to prove causes of results.[79]

It is widely known that the average IQ is about fifteen points higher among whites than blacks. However, what is not widely known is that in children before four years of age, there is no difference in IQs between blacks and whites. Yet, as they age, the IQs of blacks usually decrease while

74. Dubois, *Souls of Black Folk*, 45–46.
75. Douglass, "Self-Made Men," 136.
76. Sowell, *Intellectuals and Race*, 17–18.
77. Sowell, *Intellectuals and Race*, 7.
78. Sowell, *Intellectuals and Race*, 13.
79. Sowell, *Intellectuals and Race*, 56.

the IQs of whites remain the same.[80] Nevertheless, some argue that intelligence cannot be affected by what a person does, but is due largely to genetics. This does not mean that people cannot add information to their brains at any point of their existence. What is meant by intelligence is mental acuity or smartness. It is the type of intelligence that predicts how well one will do educationally or in other areas of complexity in their future.[81]

One of the more articulate arguments that IQs are largely genetically acquired is found in Richard J. Herrnstein and Charles Murray's *The Bell Curve*. Although Herrnstein and Murray set forth that intelligence is mainly the product of genes, even they do not deny that quite a bit may be developed by environmental factors. They stated that "even the highest estimates of heritability leave 20 to 30 percent of cognitive ability to be shaped by the environment" and went further to say that others "argue that the right proportion is 50 to 60 percent."[82] Since studies have shown that IQ is somewhat established somewhere around six years of age, Herrnstein and Murray propose that "any intervention designed to increase intelligence (or change any other basic characteristic of the child) must start early, and the earlier the better."[83] Hence, although the whole premise of *The Bell Curve* falls on the three principles that intellectual differences exist between various races and groups, much of the intellectual differences between individuals is inherited, and intelligence affects how successful one will become in society, the book need not consign any one race or individual to life on the lowest plane.[84] If intelligence can be affected at all, people can be improved upon. Just because some things are the way they are today does not mean that a greater tomorrow cannot be made for any one group or individual.

James Dobson agrees with Herrnstein and Murray that intelligence of individuals can be affected during the early years of life. He teaches that there is proof that proper "intellectual stimulation" during the first three to four years of life activates "enzyme systems" that could affect the lifelong intelligence of the individual. If this does not take place, the person may not thrive to the potential that he or she could have attained.[85] Therefore, the absence of proper prenatal vitamins and the stimulating environment

---

80. Sowell, *Intellectuals and Race*, 74–75.

81. Herrnstein and Murray, *Bell Curve*, 19–21.

82. Herrnstein and Murray, *Bell Curve*, 390.

83. Herrnstein and Murray, *Bell Curve*, 402–3.

84. Herrnstein and Murray, *Bell Curve*, 22–23, 155–56, 269–70.

85. Dobson, *Complete Marriage and Family Home Reference Guide*, 131.

of language, activities, and learning tools that are the norm in middle class and upper class households during preschool years critically affect children of lower classes who through either ignorance or lack of resources do not or cannot provide these things for their children. Upper class women tend to respond differently than lower class women when they find that they are pregnant. For upper class women, nutrition, the things they allow in their bodies, and the choice of their doctors all become major ordeals. After birth, the child is intellectually stimulated almost immediately. She almost always breastfeeds and has various toys around that are not just designed to occupy the child but to occupy him or her with a purpose. The lower classes are less concerned with the intelligence of the child or the child's future.[86] Great evidence seems to exist that intelligence can be affected in children if the right resources are deployed early in life. As well, the stability and expectations of the home environment has much to do with the emotional stability and the success of older children and young adults.

Thus, there is great evidence that what is considered to be black culture has a negative effect on the intellectual environment of black children. Some attribute this decrease in educational accomplishments to American of African descent students as not wanting to be accused of "acting white" if they do well.[87] John McWhorter chronicled an anti-intellectual bias in the black community and the charge of acting white in his book *Winning the Race: Beyond the Crisis in Black America*. McWhorter related that there was no anti-intellectual bias throughout and directly after the Civil War because blacks saw learning as a privilege. At that time, no academic gulf between blacks and whites existed. However, when segregation ended and both races attended some of the same schools, blacks seemed to set themselves against whites, and doing well in school for black boys and girls became viewed as disloyalty to the race. Because of racial peer pressure, few wanted to be seen as outside the race.[88]

Therefore, the environment in which black children are reared may greatly affect their cognitive development.[89] Adding support to this is the fact that American of African descent orphans who are adopted and socialized within white families tend to have higher IQs than other blacks.[90]

86. Murray, *Coming Apart*, 39, 41.

87. Sowell, *Intellectuals and Race*, 74–77.

88. McWhorter, *Winning the Race*, 268–69.

89. Sowell, *Intellectuals and Race*, 75.

90. Sowell, *Intellectuals and Race*, 79.

Therefore, rather than accepting the assumption that the negative conditions of many Americans of African descent today are a result of institutional racism that still pervades society, there is evidence that much of it depends on the environment in which one is socialized. So what type of environments are Americans of African descent being socialized in today? Are they socialized in environments that support the American Dream? Based on their environments, what types of results can they expect?

Chapter 2

Self-Perceptions

There is evidence that parents not only pass genetic material to their off-spring, they also transmit a certain environmental culture.[1] No person is born into this world absent from context. Families, communities, cities, states, and countries all add context to one's life. As well, communities and groups within those other subsets to which a person identifies add additional context. Each person makes a choice, to a greater or lesser extent, either to accept the identity of his or her family, group, and/or culture or rebel in some shape or form. However, as long as a human is a thinking individual, it is impossible to be unaffected by one's context.

There is a subculture within the larger United States culture that is considered to be black culture. Although many have become wealthy by glamorizing what is considered to be black culture and maintain that propagating it through movies, music, and other venues is innocuous, it has proven to be an impediment to societal success for Americans of African descent. As long as this idea of black culture is embraced and celebrated, it will keep Americans of African descent from attaining to the true goal of the Civil Rights movement, which is equality in all areas of society, and will aid in the self-destruction of black flourishing.[2]

---

1. Sowell, *Intellectuals and Race*, 83.
2. McWhorter, *Losing the Race*, x, 51.

The Historical Record

In earlier times, slavery existed in just about every country in the world, including those in Africa.[3] Hence, although American slavery had its distinctive properties, it was by no means a new invention. Muslim Arabs were among the first to engage in an intercontinental slave trade, and the Portuguese followed close behind. However, it was the trans-Atlantic slave trade from about 1550 until 1870 that brought approximately eleven million Africans to the New World and other European lands. During the grueling month-long voyage from Africa to America called the Middle Passage, over 15 percent of those transported died of disease, suicide, or were killed during insurrections. The harshness of the conditions of slavery in the New World often depended on the demand for goods and services the slaves produced. As they began to forge their own identity in the New World, the slaves retained some of the traditions from their lives in Africa, released others, and adopted new ones, concurrently with adapting to the conditions thrust upon them by the institution of slavery.[4]

When blacks were released from slavery at the end of the Civil War, Booker T. Washington testified that many former slaves left for a short time to test their freedom, but then returned to their old masters and worked out some type of agreement to stay on their land in return for work.[5] Job opportunities for former slaves were not abundant at that time. Having never experienced freedom, many former slaves had no direction. A further obstacle was added when the South passed laws called Black Codes, which denied rights to black laborers, effectively placing them back into slavery-like conditions. Hence, in 1867, in opposition to the South's recalcitrance, Reconstruction Acts legislation was passed that essentially forced civil rights for blacks. During this period, Americans of African descent served in public capacities as governor, state, and federal legislature, as well as other elected posts. However, this period did not last. In an attempt to maintain a disputed presidency, the South was freed of federal troops in what has been called the Compromise of 1877.[6]

After this, conditions hardened for Americans of African descent. The proliferation of Jim Crow laws enacted after Reconstruction where facilities

3. Franklin and Moss, *From Slavery to Freedom*, 27.

4. Henretta and Brody, *America: A Concise History*, 21, 76–82.

5. Washington, *Up from Slavery*, 24.

6. Henretta and Brody, *America*, 439, 445–46, 451, 460–61.

were kept separate for blacks and whites became pervasive in the South, and *Plessy v. Ferguson* of 1896 made segregation a federal right.[7] Although the fight for equal rights for black Americans continued throughout this time, activity intensified in 1955 when Rosa Parks, a black woman who was a long-term member of the National Association for the Advancement of Colored People (NAACP), refused to relinquish her bus seat to a white man in Montgomery, Alabama. With the emergence of the leadership of Martin Luther King Jr., the Civil Rights movement was in full swing. For 381 days, King and his supporters boycotted the bus system until the Supreme Court ruled in November of 1956 in favor of the Montgomery boycott workers. After this, various types of nonviolent protests were organized to attain the full rights of Americans of African descent.[8] Subsequently, the Civil Rights Act of 1964 was passed and forbade discrimination in educational facilities, hiring practices in workplace settings, voting facilities, and granted equal access to all public places.[9]

The legislation was the foundation for equal rights for black Americans, but there was still much work to be done. As long as sinful human beings exist in the world, prejudice—racial or otherwise—will never be totally eradicated from the human heart. Thus, the fight for equal opportunities for all Americans continues. However, to deny that America has made great progress toward this goal for every human being is simply a distorted view of reality. The fact that any American, including Americans of African descent, can protest freely without molestation proves that the America of today is quite different from the America during the heart of the Civil Rights movement. John McWhorter pointed out that most of the assumptions made by Americans of African descent that lead them to the conclusion that blacks in the United States are still greatly oppressed, and thus victims, are based on "myths" of exaggerated claims of racism and distorted perceptions about the historical record.[10] Today, there are no opportunities available to any other racial group that are not also available to Americans of African descent. Yes, people who begin with greater resources have greater opportunities because of those resources. But, it is simply illegal to refuse opportunities to a person simply because of his or her race. Americans of African descent serve or have served in just about

---

7. Cornelison and Yanak, *Great American History Fact-Finder*, 269.

8. Henretta and Brody, *America*, 818–20.

9. Cornelison and Yanak, *Great American History Fact-Finder*, 94.

10. McWhorter, *Losing the Race*, 25.

every area of the American social structure from being president of the United States to being the premier golfer in the world.

Since Americans of African descent, as a race, seem to be at the lower end of the spectrum when compared to other races in areas such as wealth, home ownership, education, and crime issues, it is assumed that the problems lie in the social structure of the United States rather than something inherent within the socialization processes of the black community itself.[11] Thus, it is often maintained that Americans of African descent still have less rights in the above-mentioned areas than other racial groups.[12] The term "institutional racism" is used to define the type of racism Americans of African descent face in the United States today. It is not the overt racism of the few that took place during Jim Crow but it is rather described as discrimination ingrained in society whereby Americans of African descent do not begin with a level playing field and are not given fair treatment.[13]

Some even attempt to justify the riots that occurred in places like Ferguson, Missouri, after the Michael Brown shooting of 2014 and in Los Angeles after four officers were acquitted of the beating of Rodney King in 1992. Although the violence that accompanied the riots is rarely justified by its commentators, it is minimized because it represents the years of "pent-up anger at a system decidedly against them, a system that has told them they are less than human for years."[14] In other words, since blacks are victims of society, they should be free from the liability of their actions in these types of situations.[15] Erica J. Wilkins, *et al.*, maintains that this mental state in Americans of African descent should be recognized as "trauma" from "the residual effects of slavery."[16] In other words, the pathologies experienced by Americans of African descent today can be traced back to the institution of slavery. In a way that is similar to what others experience in Post-Traumatic Stress Syndrome after wars or other traumatic incidents, Americans of African descent experience "Post-Traumatic Slave Syndrome," regardless of whether they were directly exposed to the institution or not.[17] Thus, "rage

11. Patrick, "Outsiders Insiders," 106.

12. Patrick, "Outsiders Insiders," 107.

13. MacPherson, "The Stephen Lawrence Inquiry," 6.5, 6.7.

14. Cunha, "Ferguson: In Defense of Rioting."

15. McWhorter, "*Losing the Race*," 65.

16. Wilkins, Whiting, Watson, Russon, and Moncrief, "Residual Effects of Slavery," 14.

17. Wilkins, Whiting, Watson, Russon, and Moncrief, "Residual Effects of Slavery,"

and passivity," "cultural mistrust," and a reluctance to "challenge the system of oppression that affects themes of powerlessness, family organization, and loss" can all be traced to Post-Traumatic Slave Syndrome.[18]

Robert H. Bork recounted how in the late 1960s and early 1970s while he was a professor at Yale, students and young adults conducted demonstrations, burned university buildings, and disrupted the entire educational environment with impunity. Yet this was not done by black or Hispanic underprivileged youth who were being unjustly targeted by the system. Many of these youths came from affluent, well-to-do white families. They refused to serve during the draft, propounded the evils of capitalism (the very ideology that made them well-off), and battled against any authoritative establishment in society. Even though these radicals verbally expressed the equality of all humans, they actually violently opposed everyone who disagreed with their rhetoric. How did the faculties and leaders respond to these rebels? For the most part, they acquiesced to the demands of the radicals and failed to hold them accountable. Now these former agitators are among today's liberal leaders: professors, politicians, journalists, and entertainers.[19]

Allowing aberrant behavior as an acceptable expression for rage is a play on the victim mentality. Is it true that Americans of African descent still experience substantial effects of slavery 150 years after slavery and psychological trauma 50 years after the Civil Rights Act was passed, or are these excuses that are allowed to go unchecked because of political correctness or not wanting to be labeled as prejudicial? Things have changed substantially since Jim Crow was made unconstitutional. Today, less than a quarter of blacks live in poverty while over half did in 1960.[20] As mentioned earlier, there is no area in politics, business, education, entertainment, or any other public enterprise that is off limits to Americans of African descent. If a person of any race begins life in a poor family with limited vocabulary and little resources, it may be much more difficult for him or her to become successful, but it can still happen with hard work. The American Dream does not promise that everybody will begin with the same resources. No person can choose the family, community, or race into which he or she will be

---

18.

18. Wilkins, Whiting, Watson, Russon, and Moncrief, "Residual Effects of Slavery," 18–19.

19. Bork, *Slouching Towards Gomorrah*, 36–51.

20. McWhorter, *Losing the Race*, 8.

born. People who can afford better homes should be able to buy them and people who can afford a private education for their children should not be hindered from doing so. However, the American Dream means that no one should be limited in any area of public life by his or her ancestral pedigree.

Bork certified that there are two ideologies on which modern liberalism are founded: "radical egalitarianism" and "radical individualism."[21] Bork defined "radical egalitarianism" as "the equality of outcomes rather than of opportunities" and "radical individualism" as "the drastic reduction of limits to personal gratification."[22] The kernel of Bork's argument was that this particular worldview is exchanging traditional American values and culture for one that actually destroys true liberty by forcing equal results (egalitarianism) and ignores what is best for society today and in the future by setting aside traditional societal morals (individualism).[23] Although both ideological agendas are being propagated by the political Left more than ever,[24] it is on the basis of egalitarianism that intellectuals assume that discrimination exists in the black community.

It is a mistake to assume that just because various racial groups tend to fall behind others in wealth, educational attainment, and other areas that the source of these diverse results is some type of discrimination against the race.[25] Thomas Sowell highlighted the fact that, regardless of the innate capabilities of a person or a people group, there are certain conditions that will inhibit flourishing. Any people group that is isolated from others or in some way limits itself through certain ideologies will limit its own potential for growth, regardless of inward potentialities or outward discrimination. Hence, even deeply ingrained traditional beliefs and practices within a cultural group can be a hindrance to growth even after all physical barriers have been eradicated.[26] Sowell went on to point out that although there is no scientific evidence that the inequalities in results among races are caused by discrimination, these assumptions are rarely challenged among

---

21. Bork, *Slouching Towards Gomorrah*, 5.

22. Bork, *Slouching Towards Gomorrah*, 5.

23. Bork, *Slouching Towards Gomorrah*, 5.

24. Bork argues on page 7 of *Slouching Towards Gomorrah* that radical egalitarianism and radical individualism are so mainstream because they are endorsed by society's movers and shakers like liberal politicians, those who practice the arts, the intellectual elite, and the press. These are they who create culture and shape reality for many Americans.

25. Sowell, *Intellectuals and Race*, 17–18.

26. Sowell, *Intellectuals and Race*, 10–19.

the intellectual elites.[27] When writers claim that some type of institutional racism or other societal obstructions are the real culprit behind black flourishing, they rarely specifically identify what those obstructions are. There is more proof that socialization factors indigenous to black culture are causing those undesirable results.

Viewing the Predominant Culture

As mentioned earlier, if any minority group is to be successful in the major culture, they must, to some extent, learn and accommodate to the major culture's standards of business. People from any other country can relocate to the United States, never learn the language, and still make a living as long as they remain predominately within their own cultural group. However, if they want to be successful in the major society, they have to learn how to communicate effectively and submit to the majority's standards of business and commerce. Many Americans of African descent are being taught to oppose the predominate culture, and this attitude is having its effects on their ability to fit in and flourish. This is not an appeal for Americans of African descent to put aside all the distinctive practices of their culture. The abundance of cultures and an appreciation for them is one of the very features that add to the richness of this country. Yet, many Americans of African descent do not see their culture as one that must fit in and coexist under the umbrella of the larger culture but most often they see the predominant culture as one to be resisted.

Simply put, the predominant culture is seen by many Americans of African descent as "white culture."[28] White culture is often characterized pejoratively among Americans of African descent; hence, blacks will do whatever it takes to disassociate themselves from white culture. McWhorter refers to this state of mind that "reinforces one's sense of psychological legitimacy, via defining oneself against an oppressor characterized as eternally depraved" as "therapeutic alienation."[29] The foundation of therapeutic alienation in the black community is "defiance," a rebellion against what is considered the white establishment because it is forever the reason for the

27. Sowell, *Intellectuals and Race*, 17–18, 50–51.
28. McWhorter, *Losing the Race*, 51.
29. McWhorter, *Winning the Race*, 6.

pathologies Americans of African descent experience today.[30] This has now largely become what it means to be black.[31]

Any American of African descent who strives to do well in school and who speaks standard English is often accused by other blacks of trying to be white. Furthermore, having a prison record is frequently considered to be a badge of authenticity for black men.[32] A prison record, an inability to speak standard English, and a failure to finish high school make it astronomically more difficult to attain a well-paying job and to do well in the majority culture. The hip hop fashion that many Americans of African descent wear is often sloppy and imitates prison clothing.[33] It is often said by black men that they cannot get ahead because nobody will give them a break. Yet, people make or break themselves by their historical record: criminal history, work record, educational resume, and financial history. A well-known axiom is that actions have consequences. A criminal record, a failure to complete school, and an inability to communicate effectively show a pattern that usually leads to degeneracy. Employers want to have successful businesses; they do not want to deal with drama. There are too many people who do not possess a sordid past who can be hired by an employer. Thus, why take a chance on somebody who has shown to make bad choices?

James Davidson Hunter explained something close to what McWhorter called therapeutic alienation by the French word "ressentiment." Ressentiment was used by Friedrich Nietzsche to include what the English word resentment means but "also involves a combination of anger, envy, hate, rage, and revenge as the motive for political action."[34] The ressentiment felt and expressed is founded in some type of perceived harm inflicted on the group by the object of the group's ressentiment. Hence, the group that expresses the ressentiment feels some sense of entitlement due to the perceived injury.[35] Although Hunter used this word as one motive in the expression of political power by liberal and conservative Christians against one another, this word also explains the victim mentality expressed by Americans of African descent. Since it is perceived that white America has wronged blacks in the past through slavery and Jim Crow laws and in

30. McWhorter, *Winning the Race*, 159, 163–64.
31. McWhorter, *Winning the Race*, 261.
32. Williams, *Enough*, 90–92, 121.
33. Williams, *Enough*, 36.
34. Hunter, *To Change the World*, 107.
35. Hunter, *To Change the World*, 107.

the present through institutional racism, white America is in a continual state of owing black Americans. Black Americans, due to this ressentiment, are justified in their anger and rage and whites should show their remorse and repentance by forever trying to make up for this injustice. So what could settle the score? Could the payment of reparations, in some form or another, settle the score? Should race-based affirmative action continue indefinitely to settle the score? There is no consensus among blacks about what should be paid or how it should be paid. It is a fact that injustice took place. Yet, will any form of payment be good enough? This all goes back to the contemporary attitude of defiance for the sake of defiance in the black community. This defiance does not make things better; it actually sabotages black lives, communities, and families.

The Pursuit of Power and Respect

Everybody wants to feel powerful. Parents want their power to be respected by their children and bosses want their power to be respected by their employees.[36] Although power is easy to recognize, it is difficult to define. In its simplest sense, power is the capacity to control or influence people, things, and/or circumstances.[37] Yet power, in a sociological sense, can be exercised in at least three distinct ways. First, one can be made to comply by force. The three sub-forms of this type of compulsion power are physically forcing compliance, controlling through threats, and withholding something the person needs. Second, people are expected to submit to the power of legitimate authority. Police, parents, teachers, and bosses exercise this type of power. Third, one can be convinced to comply either through superior arguments or out of simple respect for another individual. This is the power of influence.[38] However, a person can possess power in one area like legitimate authority and still remain powerless. For example, the boss who loses the ability to direct the affairs of his subordinates because the boss's superordinate overrules every directive he or she sets in place is effectively made powerless. In this way, a person's power is suppressed. However, a person or a group of people can also choose to be powerless by refusing to use the tools at their disposal. Hence, through their inaction, they defer

36. Lee, *Power Principle*, 1.
37. Dobson, *Complete Marriage and Family Home Reference Guide*, 216.
38. Fortunati, "Media Between Power and Empowerment," 173.

power to others. In the latter example, the only suppression on the person or group is their own refusal to choose to be powerful.

The claim of victimology is a claim of powerlessness, to some extent, and this claim is a choice.[39] When a person says that he or she is powerless to change his or her condition because of certain controls that are in place, he or she is choosing to be powerless. When a person or group feels as though success is out of their hands unless they are given some type of handicap, they choose to be powerless.[40] In other words, they give up. If a person cannot change the situation, he or she can change his or her attitude about the situation.[41] Thus, people choose to be powerful when they take charge of circumstances. For example, even in those circumstances where people are really victims, like children born into poverty and/or abusive situations, those children can continue to lament their unfortunate circumstances as they mature and remain victims or they can choose to take charge of their lives and build a better future for themselves and their future offspring. In every negative circumstance, there should be a time to grieve the loss. However, if a person never moves to the next stage, he or she will lose hope and settle into a depressive state.[42] It is important for Americans of African descent to grieve their loss and accept where they are today, but then they must rebuild. They must be offered hope that things can change when proper principles are practiced. The message that victimology relates is that Americans of African descent are victims of their circumstances and things will never get better. One can rebuild with help, but the center of the rebuilding process must come from the individuals themselves. A person with any form of dependency can be put in the best drug rehabilitation center in the world, but if the person does not put forth the necessary effort to take charge of his or her own recovery, he or she will remain an addict.

Because Americans of African descent often feel powerless due to accepting the victim mentality, they give up their right to be powerful by conventional standards and attempt to gain power by other means. One example is Malcolm Little. Little went to school in Mason, Michigan, near Lansing, during the 1940s. Since he was reared in the North, he attended school with white students. He claimed to be one of the most intelligent students in his school. However, one day in the eighth grade, his English

39. Lee, *Power Principle*, 19–21.

40. Lee, *Power Principle*, 22.

41. Lee, *Power Principle*, 47.

42. Adams, *Christian Counselor's Manual*, 375.

teacher asked him what he wanted to be when he grew up. Other students, who were not doing as well as Little in academics, desired lofty occupations. When it came to Little, he was not sure what he wanted to be, but he told the teacher that he wanted to be a lawyer. The teacher responded that "niggers" do not become lawyers so he should consider an occupation where he worked with his hands. This discouraged young Malcolm Little. From that point forward, Little accepted the powerlessness his teacher suggested, dropped out of school, and turned to a life of crime. It was in prison that he was introduced to the Nation of Islam, where he later would be known as Malcolm X.[43] In the above example, Malcolm X gave up seeking the American Dream and chose to rebel against societal norms, first through crime and then through ideological racism. He chose to accept the powerlessness his teacher placed on him and sought power through alternative venues.

Because they are told through the victim mentality that they are not as good as everybody else, many Americans of African descent have also rejected the traditional paths to power and have sought other means. Dwight N. Hopkins asserts that black men are socialized in America as inferior to whites, hence their patriarchal and aberrant attitudes in family situations are due to their pent-up hostilities toward white men.[44] However, this is a mere assumption. One can always blame someone or something else for his or her woes, but the fact is that just about anyone, unless he is truly hindered by severe retardation or such, can do better with hard work. The Bible says, "All hard work brings a profit, but mere talk leads only to poverty."[45]

Others claim that American of African descent men remain powerless due to the continuing effects of slavery, a family system that is headed mainly by women, and an economic system that oppresses them. Since they do not conform to the Western understanding of masculinity, American of African descent males were not really considered men in America until the image of Malcolm X provided a new model for black masculinity. Today, many black males are influenced by hip hop fashion, language, and style. The introduction of both Malcolm X and hip hop served the same purpose for black males. They created more confident and assertive generations of black men who always seem to be angry at the system.[46] Hence, the black man's identity seems to be tied up with anger, rage, and defiance against

43. X and Haley, *Autobiography of Malcolm X* , 35–38.
44. Hopkins, "New Black Heterosexual Male," 218.
45. Proverbs 14:23, New International Version.
46. Bush and Bush, "God Bless the Child Who Got His Own," 2–3.

American norms.[47] Although this rage and defiance created a new model for manhood and power for many black males, it failed to create the model for manhood necessary for upward mobility. As Clyde W. Franklin asserts, "the Black man presently being recognized by mainstream society is not the Black man who invented the cotton gin; he is not the Black man who pioneered the development of blood transfusions; he is not the Black man who performed miracles with the peanut; he is not the Black man who fought tirelessly for civil rights and women's rights in the 1800s."[48] In other words, the modern model for black masculinity is not having its desired effect.

The Current Definition of Blackness

Franklin proposed that American of African descent males develop their worldviews through being socialized in three areas, which he called their "primary group," their "peer group," and "mainstream society."[49] This can probably be applied to all human groups as well. The primary group is the family unit. As mentioned earlier, the family unit where a biological mother and father both raise children in one household is rare in black American families. Thus, the peer and mainstream societal groups may, by default, take on greater socializing influences for black males in today's society in the development of their ideas of masculinity. Since the father is most often absent from black homes, models of masculinity are sought and found elsewhere. Franklin asserts that when black males get their models of masculinity from peer groups, those models often include "aggressiveness, violence, competitiveness, heterosexuality, cool poses, dominance, sexism, and passive indifference in mainstream society."[50] This is epitomized in violence and gang association. The mainstream influence is media. Franklin contends that the mainstream media portrays black men as "roving, irresponsible predators" and are therefore seen as "outside of mainstream society."[51] Whether or not this is true is not the point. The question must be asked if whether Americans of African descent are setting themselves out-

47. McWhorter, *Winning the Race*, 173–74.

48. Franklin, "Men's Studies, the Men's Movement, and the Study of Black Masculinities," 11.

49. Franklin, "Men's Studies, the Men's Movement, and the Study of Black Masculinities," 12.

50. Franklin, "Men's Studies," 15.

51. Franklin, "Men's Studies," 17.

side of mainstream society with their rage, defiance, and refusal to accept mainstream norms and thus reinforcing negative stereotypes. Once again, this is an attempt to gain power in a society where power is not gained by intimidation and bullying but through holding powerful positions in societal institutions.[52]

Maintaining blackness is important to Americans of African descent. Doing well educationally, speaking standard English, dressing according to business standards, and doing things together as family have been seen by many Americans of African descent pejoratively, as acting white. McWhorter states that the fear that many Americans of African descent have of being accused of acting white is based on the idea that a black person who, in their opinion, acts white feels that he or she is better than other blacks.[53] Hence, the underlying message of this thought is that many Americans of African descent feel that the predominant culture, in some way, is better than black culture but yet they look down on other blacks who live according to that better culture. The obvious conclusion is that everybody recognizes that what is referred to as black culture is inimical to positive development. The truth is that living according to hip hop culture adds nothing to true blackness. A person is black in accordance with racial nomenclature. However, this is not how many Americans of African descent see it.

As mentioned earlier, blackness was defined by some during the Civil Rights movement in reference to the black pride taught by Malcolm X and others holding similar ideologies. Possibly because they did not feel as though they were fully accepted, many blacks did not want to be identified with white America and the things they valued.[54] However, blackness today is often defined in accordance with another form of defiance, hip hop. Hip hop has influenced language, styles of dress, and attitudes.[55] Hip hop has basically created contemporary black culture, thus a person is considered to be in conformity to blackness to the extent that he or she adapts to hip hop culture.

P. Khalil Saucier and Tryon P. Woods suggest that hip hop culture was developed in opposition to the racism ingrained in American society. It is a reaction against the continuing state of oppression and "anti-black

52. Franklin, "Men's Studies," 18.
53. McWhorter, *Losing the Race*, 148.
54. Dyson, *Between God and Gangsta Rap*, xii.
55. Bush and Bush, "God Bless the Child Who Got His Own," 3.

violence" directed toward Americans of African descent, even if it is expressed in self-destructive behavior like sexism against women and black
men killing other black men.[56] Saucier and Woods are correct in asserting
that hip hop culture is an expression of defiance, but to infer that the acting
out of self-destructive behavior is caused by some continuing oppression
against Americans of African descent makes no sense. Saucier and Woods
debunk arguments that hip hop is influencing black youths toward a path
of self-sabotage through celebrating criminal behavior and misogyny because those arguments do not take into account that hip hop is "counter
violence" due to the violence perpetrated toward the community.[57] Even if
Saucier and Woods' premise was correct, self-destructive behavior is certainly not the answer to violence carried out against a victim. Who would
agree that voluntary promiscuity is an acceptable response of a woman who
was raped and abused?

Today, however, many Americans of African descent are angry without a cause. Although President Abraham Lincoln's purpose in fighting the
Civil War was not to release the slaves but a desire to keep unity in the
Union,[58] the Civil War was still the bloodiest war the United States ever
fought.[59] Part of America's judgment for her sins of slavery was the shed-
ding of blood of her own sons during the Civil War. And although Jim Crow
was still in effect one hundred years after American slavery ended, America
tried to make it right through affirmative action and the Civil Rights Act
of 1964.[60] Today, Americans of African descent have equal access by law
to any area or position in society from the White House to the halls of
academia. The bottom line is that without the claim of institutional racism
and systemic oppression, Americans of African descent have to deal with
their own cultural failures. They are angry for anger's sake. By perpetuating
the myth of continual black oppression, they can avoid dealing with their
own problems and push the blame elsewhere.[61]

56. Saucier and Woods, "Hip Hop Studies in Black," 278.
57. Saucier and Woods, "Hip Hop Studies in Black," 280–81, 285.
58. Douglass, "Oration in Memory of Abraham Lincoln," 61–64.
59. Henretta and Brody, *America*, 408.
60. Henretta and Brody, *America*, 866.
61. McWhorter, *Winning the Race*, 163–64.

Self-Perceptions of Americans of African Descent

The emergence of hip hop has created a new model of blackness. It was built upon the earlier model of blackness set in place during the Civil Rights movement, made in opposition to the dominant culture. The Black Power ideology emerged from the radical wing of the Civil Rights movement. Many Americans of African descent observed the violence directed toward blacks and felt that nonviolent activists, like Martin Luther King Jr., did not go far enough. Hence, black militancy, in the presence of Malcolm X (spokesman for the Nation of Islam), Stokely Carmichael (chairman of the Student Nonviolent Coordinating Committee or the SNCC), and the Black Panther Party for Self Defense rose to prominence. It is important to note that these groups were formed in opposition to the oppression and violence committed against Americans of African descent during that time, which were very real.[62] It can be debated as to how much the militant wing of the Civil Rights movement accomplished in opposition to nonviolent proponents, but it is clear that the ideology of the militant wing of the Civil Rights movement still exists today and was built upon to help create the militant defiance against the broader culture that is seen today in hip hop. The difference is that the militancy of the Civil Rights movement had a real enemy on which to build; the militancy of today is opposing a phantom.

Now, young black youths live in a world with a phantom oppressor created by race-baiters and capitalized upon by the hip hop industry and black intellectuals for financial gain.[63] This ideology espoused by black intellectuals, entertainers, and others egg on many who wholeheartedly embrace the culture to continue down a slippery slope where everything inimical to human flourishing is celebrated and encouraged.[64] The intellectuals and entertainers are getting rich off of this culture, while the young men and women on the street are being entangled in a web of crime, poverty, and brokenness from which it is very difficult to escape. If these intellectuals and entertainers really cared about the black community, they would redirect the behavior of those who idolize them from this degen-

62. Joseph, "Black Power Movement," 752–62.

63. Williams, *Enough*, 26–27, 133–34, 213–14. Many on the Left shift the blame for the many issues in the black community to racism. Racism will always exist as long as humans are sinful, yet opportunities are greater today for blacks than ever before. Emphasis should be shifted from dwelling on past problems to taking advantage of present opportunities.

64. McWhorter, *Winning the Race*, 184.

eracy to a more positive direction. On the other hand, many whites are afraid to speak against the vile and degrading aspects of hip hop culture in order not to be branded racist.

Regardless of whether art reflects life or life reflects art, the minds of Americans of African descent are affected by rap music. Rap musicians are the accepted philosophers in much of the black community. In defense of the hip hop culture, Michael Eric Dyson asserts that the attitude gained by many blacks is an attempt to "keep it real" by embracing a ghetto mentality in opposition to the "unreal bourgeois black" who accepts American mainstream culture. Hence, as Dyson purports, "the quest for the Real Black Person was initially set in motion by black folk defending themselves against the rigid rule of white stereotype and the suffocating effect of white prejudice."[65] However, the gangsta persona, the misogynistic lyrics, and the glamorization of ghetto life actually enforce stereotypes that make other Americans afraid of blacks and young blacks idolize this behavior that will never bring success in mainstream society.[66] Many rap artists are doing well, at least financially. They can afford a felony on their record because they have millions of dollars to help them live above the stigma. However, that is not so for the young black male who tries to imitate what he sees rappers portray. Life gets astronomically more difficult for the young black youth who fails to finish school, gets a prison record, or joins a gang.[67] Rap artists can decorate their bodies and faces with tattoos and, with their millions, live above what are accepted business practices. But the young black youths who tattoo themselves on their public areas like their faces or with derogatory slogans may have a more difficult time finding a well-paying job. Rap artists can boast of their masculinity and all the women they impregnate because they can afford the child support. Yet the young black male who leaves a string of children born out of wedlock will have a hard time getting ahead financially and do a severe disservice to those women and their fatherless children.[68]

Juan Williams likened the greed of the hip hop business to that of slavery because, in a similar way to how the "cheap labor" of slavery was

65. Dyson, *Between God and Gangsta Rap*, xii.

66. McWhorter, *Winning the Race*, 315–18, 322.

67. Hattery and Smith, "Families of Incarcerated African American Men," 141. Hattery and Smith state that almost one-third of black males will spend time incarcerated and that most employers check criminal records before they hire.

68. Hattery and Smith, "Families of Incarcerated African American Men," 139. Nearly 40 percent of single mothers live in poverty.

economically fruitful to southern plantation owners, the white owners of record labels today are benefiting off of young blacks wanting to make names for themselves.[69] On a similar note, the hip hop rappers and black producers can be compared to drug dealers and pimps. The drug dealer knowingly sells something dangerous to his community to make financial gain. He justifies himself because people freely buy what he has to offer. The consumers want what they sell. Pimps degrade women (and these days, men) to make wealth for themselves. Yet they accept none of the responsibility for providing poison to and degrading their brothers, sisters, sons, and daughters. Even the law considers selling drugs and promotion of prostitution (pimping) to be higher penalties than possessing drugs for private use or prostituting oneself.[70] Likewise, these promoters of poison accept no responsibility for the hurt they cause to a whole race of people, whom they claim to love. Is this the reason that those who fought for equal rights for Americans of African descent risked their lives and even died?[71]

It is amazing that black intellectual leaders, like Michael Eric Dyson, can defend contemporary rap music, which is the booming voice of hip hop, when the philosophies of this lyrical genre set such negative standards for blacks. Although he condemns the sexploitation of women, the glamorization of violence, and the homophobia presented in gangsta rap, Dyson likens the militant and controversial group Public Enemy to the biblical prophet Jeremiah and praises Ice Cube, who routinely uses the n-word for fellow blacks and the b-word for women, for "rattling the pieties of the black bourgeoisie."[72] This is not a question of free speech. Like everyone else, gangsta rappers have the right to free speech, however poisonous it may be. The question is whether this philosophy that is being uncritically digested by a whole generation of Americans of African descent is inimical to the development of the community. Dyson portrays gangsta rap, with all its problems, as a medium used by youth who fail to see conventional modes of addressing community issues as suitable.[73] But other than a place to vent their frustrations, is this philosophy helping them to overcome the years of pathology the community is suffering? Do Americans of African descent see themselves as a part of America who wants the best that America has

69. Williams, *Enough*, 134.

70. "Texas Penal Code" 483.042.

71. Williams, *Enough*, 138–39.

72. Dyson, *Between God and Gangsta Rap*, 171, 173, 184.

73. Dyson, *Between God and Gangsta Rap*, 185.

to offer like stable families, solid careers, home ownership, and respectability, or do they see themselves as a subgroup that will continually remain a part of the underclass, living in ghettos as outcasts of conventional society? Healthy expectations often produce healthy results. What are Americans of African descent expecting for themselves?

The Acceptance of Degeneracy

Quite often, rap lyrics and black film romanticize criminality and gang life. The genre of rap music is not what makes today's rap wrong. It is the message.[74] The usual explanation for the vivid misogyny, the glamorization of criminal behavior and violence, and the police-hating rhetoric is that the message is supposed to be a true representation of life for poor blacks, or an attempt to "keep it real."[75] The phrase "keep it real" means that one should never forget his or her ghetto roots.[76] Yet, is that where Americans of African descent want to stay? Is it not the goal to do better for oneself, to get out of the ghetto? Are Snoop Dog, Ice Cube, or other rappers who make millions living in the hood? These philosophers of the hood paint a picture that depicts real blackness to include loose women, who they consistently refer to by derogatory names, making quick money through selling drugs, and a prison record as a rite of passage. The middle class values that if internalized by young blacks could make them successful are mocked as anti-black. Hence, these young people who are looking for models for life are pointed away from educational attainments and conventional models of success to a persona of gangs, drugs, flashy jewelry, expensive tennis shoes, and anger without a cause.[77] Dyson argues that the redeeming quality of rap is that it offers "competing visions of black identity" and "counters official versions of history with narratives from despised young folk."[78] But one must ask whether those historical narratives are correct and those competing visions of blackness helpful.

Just about any American can do well if he or she completes high school, stays away from criminal behavior, gets a career based on a college education or learning a trade, and practices responsible fiscal decisions.

74. Williams, *Enough*, 126.

75. Williams, *Enough*, 127.

76. Dyson, *Is Cosby Right?*, 37.

77. Williams, *Enough*, 140.

78. Dyson, *Is Cosby Right?*, 35.

It does not matter what a person's race is; there are examples of successful people from all walks of life. However, when bad decisions are made while a person is young, like failing to complete high school, obtaining a prison record, or becoming a teenage parent, life's options become narrower and success becomes much more difficult to attain.

When a child acts out in school, it is often attributed to the child putting up a smoke screen because he or she has not acquired the skills necessary to do the work. Hence, the child who feels powerless because of his or her inability to do the work, makes himself or herself powerful by acting out. It is a diversion from the real issue. Rap music and the hip hop industry accomplish something similar. Rappers create an over the top depiction of life that feeds male egos with images of power.[79] Many black males feed their egos by the shock and fear that others feel toward them. This fear they sense makes them feel powerful. As well, their disdain for authority also makes them feel powerful. Because they have rights, they feel that parents, teachers, and law enforcement cannot tell them what to do. It makes them feel powerful to look with disdain upon a police officer because they know that a police officer cannot legally violate their civil rights.[80] However, what they do not understand is that obedience to authority and living in harmony with those around them are skills without which few can live successfully in the United States. The refusal to develop basic skills to coexist with others different from themselves and contribute to society will ensure their continued status in the underclass. Young Americans of African descent must be taught new paths to power, paths to which successful Americans ascribe every day. Look at all the Americans of African descent who are doing well, outside of those who won the lottery or became a professional athlete. They got there by practicing good, solid business principles. Even those who do well as rappers are only successful because of their or somebody else's business prowess.

As will be discussed later, all humans are made in the image of God.[81] This gives all humans equal status in their humanity. However, partly because of a negative self-image and an ignorance of history, many Ameri-

79. McWhorter, *Winning the Race*, 334.

80. From personal knowledge as a black police officer, many Americans of African descent do not dislike only white police officers, but also show disdain for all police officers. Hence, although race may be included, the major problem is either with authority in general or anything that is a part of the system that is seen as oppressive to the black community.

81. Genesis 1:26–27.

cans of African descent engage in self-deprecating behavior. A well-known stereotype of Americans of African descent that began during the time of slavery and continued for a hundred years thereafter is that they are closer to animals and in need of the white race's supervision.[82] Even the conservative scholars C. F. Keil and F. Delitzsch held that the whole race of Hamites lean toward being immoral and that the curse of Canaan given in Genesis 9:25 applied to all Hamites, including blacks.[83] However, a truly biblical worldview of creation is that no humans evolved from lower animals; they were created in God's image. But, just as the tempter made a fool out of the first human pair by using a lower animal (a serpent) to contradict what God clearly told them, even so he is making a fool out of Americans of African descent today.[84] By putting so much emphasis on the very things that are animalistic in human nature, like sex and physical force, rather than the higher parts of human nature, like compassion and altruistic love, the tempter is leading Americans of African descent to degrade themselves and internalize negative portrayals passed on about blacks during slavery and the Jim Crow era. Americans of African descent no longer need others to invalidate and degrade their humanity; they are being deceived into invalidating and degrading themselves.

During slavery and Jim Crow, Americans of African descent were referred to as "niggers." Although the term "nigger" may have had its beginning with African slaves mispronouncing the word "negro," it became a pejorative word whereby whites identified blacks as an inferior race that needed their supervision.[85] It is amazing that people today defend using any derivative of that word as a term of endearment. Many blacks commonly refer to one another with a derivative form of nigger, or nigga. To show just how inflammatory the word still is, although black rap artists and comedians regularly use the term in their circles, they will rarely allow a white person to use the term with impunity.[86] In Malcom X's autobiography, he named a chapter "Mascot." In it, he spoke about how everybody, including teachers, referred to him as a "nigger" and/or a "coon." Now, he admits that they probably meant little harm, but he further admits that it

82. Elwang, "Negroes of Columbia, Missouri," 64.

83. Keil and Delitzsch, *Pentateuch*, 157.

84. Genesis 3:1–5.

85. Fogle, "Etymology, Evolution, and Social Acceptability of 'Nigger,' 'Negro,' and 'Nigga,'" 84–85.

86. Parks and Jones, "Nigger," 1325.

was his understanding that whites, even good white people, all considered themselves better than black people, better than niggers. Hence, although he was accepted as a "nigger," it was important that he understood that he was to keep his place.[87] Today, many Americans of African descent freely use this term for themselves and other blacks. In doing so, they set themselves apart from the larger society who are not niggers or niggas and accept for themselves all that the word had come to mean. Although some blacks may have developed a new meaning for the word among themselves, it is still one of the most offensive words in the English vocabulary, if used by a white person of a black person, because of its historical usage.

When Americans of African descent choose to do better for themselves and learn standard English, do well educationally, and assimilate into the larger society, they do not cash in their blackness card. Black people are black because they are born that way. Americans of African descent should reject the notion that blackness is a way of speech, a way of dress, a rejection of educational pursuits, and a rejection of mainstream cultural norms. Americans of African descent share a struggle, a history. They all desire the same thing: equal footing with everyone else. But they will not possess the object of their desire by shocking the conscious of the larger society through degeneracy and thus segregating themselves. It is imperative that Americans of African descent accept practices in their lives that work for their spiritual, social, and economic development. They will cross over the mountaintop by making responsible decisions and by good practical actions.

87. X and Haley, *Autobiography*, 27–30, 36.

Chapter 3

The Shared Human Experience

Some Americans of African descent purport that white people are inherently evil. The young Louis X, who would later come to be known as Louis Farrakhan, wrote a play called *The Trial* where he charged the "white man" with "being the greatest liar," "drunkard," "gambler," "peace-breaker," "adulterer," "robber," "deceiver," and "trouble-maker on earth."[1] Michael Eric Dyson said that an "overemphasis on personal responsibility," when speaking about the pathologies of Americans of African descent, "let many of these whites off the hook."[2] So why should white people be left on the hook? Should white people or America in general be forever in debt for something their forefathers did? Is it not plausible to believe that if black people were in the place of whites and whites were in the place of blacks during the founding of this country that blacks would have enslaved whites just as white people enslaved blacks? Was not slavery ubiquitous in the ancient world?

Evil is neither a black thing nor a white thing; it is a human thing. As stated earlier, the whole world of antiquity practiced slavery. During the Muslim conquest of Africa, they made personal slaves of some and acquired others for sale. Egyptians, Babylonians, Persians, Greeks, and Romans all practiced slavery.[3] Most of the Africans that were carried to the New World were gathered by other Africans, who in turn traded them

1. Lincoln, *Black Muslims in America*, 1.
2. Dyson, *Is Bill Cosby Right?*, 5.
3. Franklin and Moss, *From Slavery to Freedom*, 27–28.

in pre-established port cities.[4] Slaves were traded in Africa for goods that brought wealth and power to certain African states, and some of those African states became very powerful with the artillery they traded for slaves. The slaves were then brought to the New World where they were worked to create wealth and power for their masters.[5] Truly, "the love of money is a root of all kinds of evils."[6]

According to the Bible, all humans are sinners.[7] Hence, every human person and group is capable of great evil. No one human group is inherently more sinful than another. Each individual comes into the world as a sinner, and each group of sinners is socialized into its respective sinful environments. Yes, American slavery took on a very harsh and evil distinctive quality because it was race-based and because of the relatively inexpensive price of slaves in comparison to the amount of wealth a slave produced. However, it was the perceived need to create wealth in the New World that created the circumstances.[8]

This chapter will discuss the shared human experience. In order to understand the human experience, it is important first to understand what it means to be human. Since God is the creator of humanity, one must look to him to ascertain what humanness entails. Next, in order to live in a world of community, God established authority. Authority is not a bad thing; it is necessary to the proper working of any institution. Finally, the issue of the sinfulness of all humans will be revisited. One cannot hold another accountable for all wrongs; all humans are at fault. Humans must work together to rebuild and reestablish humanity according to its original plan.

The Biblical Idea of Humanness: Made in God's Image

If God is the creator of this universe and this universe includes human beings, it is important to look to him for what is essentially human. Things that are created or formed by intelligent beings are usually created for a purpose.[9] Lawnmowers were developed to better assist humans in cutting grass, spoons were formed to shovel food in a person's mouth, and motor

4. Henretta and Brody, *America*, 21–22.
5. Henretta and Brody, *America*, 76–77.
6. 1 Timothy 6:10.
7. Romans 3:23.
8. Henretta and Brody, *America*, 76, 81.
9. Kemper, Kemper, and Luskin, *Discovering Intelligent Design*, 10.

vehicles were assembled to help transport people and things from one place to another. Hence, it is logical to assume that if humans were created by an intelligent being, they too have a purpose. However, if humans were not created by God, then humans really have no purpose. They are simply a blob of matter that is more complex than lower forms.

This book assumes a biblical worldview. There is no scientific proof that anything containing both specificity and complexity came into being without some type of intelligence behind it.[10] Humans contain both specificity and complexity. Humans display specificity because "their structures are specially suited to perform biological processes" and complex "because their structures are highly unlikely."[11] So if humans were created to fulfill a God-ordained purpose, an unbiblical worldview of what humans ought to be will result in a warped product of humanity. This is what is happening with many people today, and especially with Americans of African descent. In this portion of this book, the idea of humanness will be discussed. If it is to be determined that many Americans of African descent should redirect their behavior, the true standard of right behavior for humanity must first be determined and accepted by the community.

What Does It Mean to Be Made in God's Image?

Before creation, God alone existed. When he created, all that comprises the physical universe came into being.[12] After bringing the physical world into form, he created sea creatures, birds, and animals "according to their kinds,"[13] but, when he made humans, he made them "in his own image."[14] Hence, a distinction was made between humans and all other creatures. Of all creation, only humans are said to be made in the image of God, and this confers on humans a dignity not conferred on any other created thing. Because of God's image in humans, the human being is the only earthly creature that has the capacity of having a personal relationship with God.[15] Because all humans are created in God's image, no person can consider another person as less of a person because he or she is black, white, Hispanic,

10. Kemper, Kemper, and Luskin, *Discovering Intelligent Design*, 19.

11. Kemper, Kemper, and Luskin, *Discovering Intelligent Design*, 20.

12. Genesis 1:1.

13. Genesis 1:21, 24, 25.

14. Genesis 1:26–27; 5:2.

15. Erickson, *Christian Theology*, 471.

mentally impaired, young, old, or still in the womb because all humans share the dignity of the image of God.

What does it mean to be made in the image of God? The Bible does not offer an overt definition. Yet it can be determined by scriptural context that to be made in the image and likeness of God means, among other things, that humans share a greater similarity to God than any other creature and represent God in relation to earthly things.[16] The image of God in humans is what separates them from all other creatures; it is essential to humanness. As Wayne Grudem explains, "both the Hebrew words 'image' (*tselem*) and 'likeness' (*demût*) refer to something that is similar but not identical to the thing it represents . . . The word 'image' can also be used of something that represents something else."[17] W. Sibley Towner pointed out that the word "image" (צֶלֶם) is used in the Hebrew Bible mainly in reference to something "carved" to look like something else, like an idol, but is also used in reference to something in the "semblance" of something else, like a shadow.[18] As well, Towner affirms that "likeness" (דְּמוּת) is more "abstract" in its usage than צֶלֶם and "can refer more to similarities other than visual ones."[19] However, although there are nuances of differences between the two words, Paul Sands expressed that the two words are used in the Old Testament in essentially a synonymous manner.[20] In Genesis 5:3, Adam is said to have fathered Seth "in his own likeness, after his image." Although God is Spirit and has no physical image,[21] he uses anthropomorphic terms of himself, expressing certain aspects of his nature. Various human body parts are referenced to God to explain his actions. In Exodus 7:5, God will "stretch out my hand against Egypt"; in Numbers 6:25, God will "make his face to shine" on his people; in Psalm 34:15, "the eyes of the LORD are toward the righteous." These are just a few examples, but they show that God is involved in some of the very acts that humans do, but God gave humans bodies to accomplish these things on a much smaller scale.

Another interesting note is Psalm 8. The psalmist asked in verse 4, "What is a man that you are mindful of him, and the son of man that you care for him?" The answer spoke first of humanity's qualitative nature in

---

16. Grudem, *Making Sense of Man and Sin*, 37, 44.

17. Grudem, *Making Sense of Man and Sin*, 37–38.

18. Towner, "Clones of God," 345–46.

19. Towner, "Clones of God," 346.

20. Sands, "*Imago Dei* as Vocation," 29.

21. Exodus 4:15–18; John 4:24.

verse 5 and then his commission as the reigning steward of God over the Earth and its creatures in verses 6–8. The English Standard Version translates the beginning of verse 5 as "Yet you made him a little lower than the heavenly beings," but the Hebrew word for "heavenly beings" is אֱלֹהִים or God. This is the same Hebrew word used for the Creator in the early chapters of Genesis and of God in general throughout the Hebrew Scriptures. Nevertheless, the Bible is not saying that humans are divinity. The fact that God is transcendent to anything created is clearly manifest in Genesis as well as the remainder of the Bible.[22] Yet, the psalmist is clearly portraying that humans are directly below God in their rule over creation on Earth. The idea presented here refers to the royal status of humanity as ruler over God's creation.[23] Humans, as royal agents, exercise the dominion of God in the Earth.[24]

Although many try to define the image of God by things such as rationality, conscience, or the like, those definitions are based on assumptions from the text. If the image of God is defined solely by function, animals and angels share various functional qualities with humans, to a lesser or greater degree.[25] What is written in the context is that humans share more of a likeness to God than any other creature and an expectation for humans to maintain the creation under God's authority. It can further be assumed as true that God would create within humanity the necessary qualities needed to properly represent him, although that is not expressly mentioned in the passage. It can only be deduced through the passage in Genesis 1 that the *imago Dei* in humans is at least partly displayed by the way they relate to God, one another, and the world they rule as God's vice-regents. Hence Sands declares that the image of God is best described as "a God-given vocation" or "a royal-functional view" based on the "tasks assigned" to humans in Genesis 1:26–28 directly after stating that they were created in the image of God.[26] The royal-functional view sets humans apart from all other creation.

Although Sands has a valid argument, Michael S. Heiser pointed out a major flaw in any view based on human aptitude. Heiser related that a fertilized egg in a womb possesses no consciousness, mental acumen,

22. Reiss, "Adam: Created in the Image and Likeness of God," 185.

23. VanGemeren, *Psalms*, 141.

24. Goldingay, *Psalms*, 159.

25. Vainio, "*Imago Dei* and Human Rationality," 123.

26. Sands, "*Imago Dei* as Vocation," 36–37.

rationality, or emotions. Hence if function alone is an indicator of the image of God, a zygote would only potentially be a person rather than a real person. The same could be said for those who are severely mentally challenged. Thus, the image of God in humans cannot be seen according to something a human can do, but it must be seen in accordance to what a human is. Hence, Heiser defines the image of God as "status" rather than "ability." Since humans represent God on Earth, "to be human is to image God."[27] Heiser's description maintains the essential elements in Sands' definition. Humanity as a group is tasked with fulfilling the vocational elements of Genesis 1:26–28. The context of Genesis 1:26–28 assumes that those participating in the image of God will, at least collectively, fulfill the vocational elements presented there.

According to Genesis 1:26 and 27, God made the man and the woman in his image and likeness before they did anything and gave them dominion over all sea creatures, birds, and animals. In these verses, God explains the tasks assigned to humans through what has been called the cultural mandate because, through them, God directed humans "to create cultures" and "build civilizations."[28] Humans were to "be fruitful and multiply and fill the earth," "subdue it (the earth)," and exercise "dominion" over all sea creatures, birds, and animals.[29] Doing this was the way humans were to glorify God as his stewards and vice-regents over his created order. When a person rules over something in another's stead as a steward, it is always understood that the delegated authority's autonomy is limited as the other's representative. In the same way, God expected humans to care for the Earth and its inhabitants in his stead and only under his direction. Although all humans, even fallen ones, participate in the image of God,[30] humans reflect that image better as they "are being transformed into the same image from one degree of glory to another" by "the Lord, who is the Spirit."[31] Hence, the image of God is better reflected as humans submit their lives to Christ.

The first essential element in the cultural mandate is to "be fruitful and multiply and fill the earth." This is essentially a directive to build strong families. When the declaration is made in Genesis 1:27 about God creating humans in his image, the change from the singular, "in the image of God he

27. Heiser, *Unseen Realm*, 41–43.

28. Pearcey, *Total Truth*, 47.

29. Genesis 1:28.

30. Genesis 9:6; James 3:9.

31. 2 Corinthians 3:18.

created him," to the plural, "male and female he created them," is important. The man was not created with both sexes; Adam was created a man. However, God took a rib out of the man to make him a suitable helper.[32] This made the woman distinct from yet equal to the man because they share the same nature, humanity.[33] Humans were not created asexual; a male and a female are required to produce offspring. However, just like God exists as plurality in oneness (i.e., the Trinity), so man (אָדָם), the singular (i.e., humanity), was made "through an expression of plurality."[34] In Genesis 1:26 the Bible affirms the plurality in the one God in the phrase, "And God said, 'Let us make man in our image, after our likeness.'" Therefore marriage, as a foundation of the family, models God. Although the man was made first in the image of God and then the woman was made from the man,[35] each person, whether male or female, represents the image of God. In 1 Corinthians 11:7, the Apostle Paul said that the man is "the image and glory of God," while the woman is "the glory of man." He did not say that the woman is the image of the man because the Bible already affirmed, in the passages mentioned above, that the woman is also the image of God.

The only thing in God's original creation that he pronounced "not good" was the man to be alone, so he made from him "a helper fit for him."[36] The Hebrew word for "helper" in this passage is עֵזֶר. The emphasis of the word is "cooperation," especially when one person's strength is inadequate. Neither a man nor a woman is adequate to be the foundation of a family by himself or herself. The word does not denote inferiority; it is used of God in the Hebrew Qal about 30 times.[37] Hence, he created the woman to be both the man's companion in life and his partner in reproduction and family building. The fact that the Bible teaches that the normal course of each family unit is for a man to "leave" the one in which he was reared, represented by his mother and father, and "hold fast" to his wife to form a new permanent family unit proves that the normal foundation of any family should be a permanent and monogamous union between one man and one

32. Genesis 2:21–22.

33. Galatians 3:28. This neither denies the different functions of the sexes (male and female) nor male headship in the marriage relationship as explained in 1 Corinthians 11:3, 7–9 and Ephesians 5:22–33.Galatians 3:28 speaks of the equality of men and women as joint-heirs in Christ.

34. Sailhamer, *Genesis-Leviticus*, 70.

35. 1 Corinthians 11:12; 1 Timothy 2:13.

36. Genesis 2:18.

37. Bergmann, עֵזֶר, 872–82.

woman. The Hebrew word for "leave" is עָזַב and the Hebrew word for "hold fast" is דָּבַק. The words denote an altering of one's priorities from parents to the wife. In ancient Israel this would have been noteworthy because one's obligations to parents fell only second to his or her obligations to God.[38] The term for "hold fast" (דָּבַק) is often used in relation to how Israel should "hold fast" to God.[39] The family was the first institution created and was intended to serve as the foundation of all other human sociological structures (communities, cities, etc.). When humans reproduce, they share in God's creative abilities, and when humans exercise dominion, they share in God's rule as his stewards and agents.[40]

The goal of the permanent union between the man and the woman forming the foundation of the new family unit is that the man and the woman become "one flesh."[41] Since God is autonomous and omnipotent, he could have created any kind of creature he chose to be the helper of man, or he could have simply created man with no need for a companion. He could have chosen an animal, another male, or something totally different. However, he must have had a really good reason in his infinite wisdom to make the woman as the only helper suitable for the man. After God created the whole Earth and all the animals, "there was not found a helper fit for him (the man)."[42] Hence, he created the woman from a part of the man. The "one-flesh" terminology is related to what the man said about the woman when she was presented to him. Adam said that the woman was "bone of my bones and flesh of my flesh," thus "she shall be called woman, because she was taken out of man."[43] God created the first pair in relation to each other, but when a man and a woman marry, a similar pattern emerges. The "leaving" of father and mother and "holding fast" to his wife in Genesis 2:24 concludes the "bone of my bone and flesh of my flesh" passage in verse 23 by introducing it with, "therefore, a man shall leave ... " Hence, the new marriage relation between the man and the woman will supersede the consanguinity relation previously enjoyed with their parents.[44] The Apostle Paul picks up on this idea in Ephesians 5:29 where he speaks about how

38. Wenham, *Genesis 1–15*, 71.
39. Wenham, *Genesis 1–15*, 71. See also Deut 10:20; 11:22; 13:5.
40. Fretheim, Brueggemann, and Kaiser, *Genesis-Leviticus*, 356.
41. Genesis 2:24.
42. Genesis 2:20.
43. Genesis 2:23.
44. Bruce Kay, "'One Flesh' and Marriage," 48.

a husband should love his wife. He said, "For no one ever hated his own flesh, but nourishes and cherishes it, just as Christ does the church." Therefore, based on the evidence presented above, the "one-flesh" relationship is one where the wife becomes an extension of the man. The two essentially become "one flesh" in forming the basis of the new household in a lifelong monogamous partnership of mutual care and companionship as well as producing and rearing children.

It should be pointed out that God blessed the human pair before he told them, "be fruitful and multiply."[45] Producing offspring is considered a blessing in the Bible. In Genesis 9:1, "God blessed Noah and his sons" before he repeated those same words, "be fruitful and multiply and fill the earth." Offspring made under the direction of God is a blessing and will make for the well-being of humanity.[46] Through the prophet Malachi, God rebuked the men of Judah for breaking the marriage covenant with their wives. Malachi said that God made the man and his wife to be one "with a portion of the Spirit in their union," and a major purpose of the union is because God sought "Godly offspring."[47] Although there are always exceptions to the rule, the Bible teaches that a good solid marriage based on the one-flesh covenant is a major contributor in producing righteous descendants. On the converse, the Bible also teaches that the breaking of the one-flesh marriage covenant is a great contributor to ungodly offspring. Jesus spoke of marriage as the "joining together" of a man and a woman by God into a one-flesh covenant relationship, and if God joined the two, humans should not have the audacity to separate them.[48] The term used for "joined together" in Matthew 19:6 is συνέζευξεν and literally means "yoked together" like two oxen sharing the same yoke to plow. Hence, Jesus' use of this term portrayed oneness in marriage as "partners working in tandem for a common cause."[49]

Since marriage makes a man and a woman "one flesh," divorce can be referred to as a type of amputation.[50] The only exception to a lifelong com-

45. Genesis 1:28.

46. Psalm 127:3–5.

47. Malachi 2:15.

48. Matthew 19:6.

49. Bloomberg, "Marriage, Divorce, Remarriage, and Celibacy," 169.

50. C. S. Lewis, *Mere Christianity*, 105. It is not the object of this work to deal with divorce. Jesus' most comprehensive teaching about the intended permanence of marriage and the possibility of divorce can be found in Matthew 19:3–12. What Jesus first makes clear in this passage is that in the original creation, "he made them male and female"

mitment between the husband and the wife offered in the Bible by Jesus was sexual immorality.[51] Although the marriage covenant is consummated and remembered through sexual union between a husband and his wife, much like Christians observe the Eucharist to remember their fellowship with Christ through his death, the one-flesh union is not limited to sex. The one-flesh union also "incorporates every aspect of intimacy and interdependence, which should ideally render the married couple a unified entity at the deepest levels of interpersonal communion."[52] However, although the one-flesh union includes more than sex, Jesus' teaching on divorce in Matthew 19:2–12 is clear that when either a husband or a wife engages in sex with another person, "he/she automatically disengages from his/her spouse and becomes 'one' with the other person."[53] Paul alludes to this in 1 Corinthians 6:15–16 when he states that sexual union with a prostitute makes a person "one body" with her, and then he loosely quotes the latter part of Genesis 2:24, "the two will become one flesh."[54] So, adultery, at least,

---

(verse 4). This sets apart the necessity of gender distinctions in the marriage covenant (thus, no homosexuality, bestiality, etc.) as well as the original intention of monogamy between the pair (thus, no polygamy, polyamory, etc.). Second, he said, "They are no longer two but one flesh" (verse 6a). Through marriage, the man and the woman are joined together to form a oneness on which to base the family. Third, Jesus concludes his argument with, "What therefore God has joined together, let not man separate" (verse 6b). Marriage is intended to be a lifelong monogamous union. Fourth, Jesus upheld that Moses permitted, rather than mandated, divorce under certain circumstances because of the sinful and stubborn hearts of humans (verse 8). Finally, the only thing that breaks that oneness bond is sexual immorality because it violates the one-flesh union (verse 9). Paul added one more ground for divorce in 1 Corinthians 7:15, desertion of a believer by an unbeliever.

51. Heth, "Jesus on Divorce," 4–29. In 1985, Heth, along with Gordon Wenham, wrote *Jesus and Divorce: The Problem with Evangelical Consensus*, which was updated in 1997 where he and Wenham argued that Jesus did not permit remarriage after divorce, under any circumstance. However, in this more recent article, Heth has reversed his view to what he calls "the majority evangelical Protestant view" (5). Although the original book presented six interpretations of Jesus' view on divorce (Matthew 5:32; 19:9), Heth stated that there are really only two accepted positions among evangelicals today: the majority view, which allows remarriage after divorce on the grounds of either adultery and/or desertion and the minority view, which allows for separation under some circumstances but rejects remarriage after divorce as long as the other party is alive. Heth testified that the overwhelming support of evangelical scholarship supports the majority view (4).

52. Bloomberg, "Marriage, Divorce, Remarriage, and Celibacy," 167.

53. Spencer, "Scripture, Hermeneutics, and Matthew's Jesus," 377.

54. F. Scott Spencer further elaborates in "Scripture, Hermeneutics, and Matthew's Jesus" that when Jesus answered the Pharisees's question about whether "it is lawful to divorce one's wife for any cause" in Matthew 19:3 and following, he referred back to the

interrupts one-flesh intimacy and, at most, destroys it. Thus, sexual laxness is both condemned and discouraged throughout the Bible because it fights against the very union that was to be the foundation of society. Strong marriages support strong families, which make strong communities. All of this is based on a sexual ethic that supports sexual expression only in the midst of a loving, faithful marital relationship between one man and one woman. Accordingly, any use of sexuality outside of God's original intention undermines proper community building. As well, any community building that does not support the family in the way God created it is community building on a shaky foundation.

The second essential element in the cultural mandate is to "subdue" the Earth. The Hebrew word for "subdue" is כָּבַשׁ, a strong word that means to "conquer" and "subjugate," thus the idea is to possess.[55] This means that humans should harvest the Earth's resources for their good but in a responsible way.[56] The natural world is the world as God created it; how humans harvested the Earth's resources has to do with the development of human cultures. In essence, culture incudes "the entire human sub-creation developed from the creation as it came from the Father's hand."[57] God supplied the Earth and its natural resources; culture is what humans made with the Earth and its natural resources. Thus, humans were mandated by God to use what he created to build structures for community living while still recognizing and maintaining a society under God's overreaching authority.

---

beginning union of the original man and woman before sin entered the picture. In that union, which should be a model for all others, God joined the man and the woman together to be "one flesh." That joining together is then consummated through the sexual union through which the act of "sexual intercourse melds two body-persons into one." Hence, adultery disrupts that "one-flesh" union. Therefore, if one of the one-flesh participants engage in sexual relations with another, he or she has become susceptible to being divorced by the innocent party. Jesus clearly manifested that "there is no such thing as casual sex in this arrangement" (376–77). However, Jesus made clear that divorce is not mandatory under such circumstances but permitted (Matt 19:7–8). The essence of the relationship between God and his imperfect and heavily flawed human creatures is that he forgives and restores the penitent and Scripture makes certain that he expects nothing less from humans. For "if you don't forgive others their trespasses, neither will your father forgive your trespasses" (Matt 6:15). However, forgiveness is one thing and restoration to one's former position is another. The injured party has the right to walk away when the one-flesh relationship has been severed through adultery, or he or she can restore the injured party and renew the one-flesh relationship.

55. Hartley, *Genesis*, 49–50.

56. Pearcey, *Total Truth*, 47–48.

57. Johnson, "Christ and Culture," 6.

Consequently, any culture building that is done outside of God's authority fights against his original plan.

The third essential element of the cultural mandate is to "have dominion" over sea creatures, birds, and animals. In other words, God desires that humans care for other living creatures responsibly. The Hebrew word for dominion is רָדָה. Both כָּבַשׁ and רָדָה can be used in the sense of a severe use of power, but the context here speaks of God sharing his power with humans by conferring on them kingly authority as God's vice-regent over the Earth.[58] Humans must care for the Earth created by God—in God's way—to promote maximum flourishing on the Earth.

To fulfill the creation mandate under God's auspices is the only way to build a solid foundation for human culture. This all goes back to the biblical teaching of God's institutional plan for the family as the venue for developing a long-lasting value system within humans. When the institution crumbles because of illegitimate births, divorce, or the wholesale change in its structure, chaos will ensue.

Sin and the Image of God

If humans are created in the image of God, then there should be a certain order and dignity to the way humans should live. The Bible exhorts humans to "be imitators of God, as beloved children."[59] Yet what should be and what is are two different things altogether. Most people in the world are not living in correlation to the creation mandate. The reason for this is the entrance of sin into the human person and environment.

The image of God was not lost in humans when sin entered the world, but it was marred.[60] However, in a dissenting point of view, John F. Kilner argues that the *imago Dei* was neither lost nor damaged due to the fall. He admits that sin has severely damaged humanity but maintains that Scripture "consistently refrains from indicating that this image has been damaged or lost."[61] Scripture clearly upholds that each person of fallen humanity is still a partaker of the image of God. Fallen humans are humans, nevertheless. Genesis 9:6 condemns the murderer to capital punishment simply because "God made man in his own image." As well, James 3:9 says

58. Towner, "Clones of God," 347.

59. Ephesians 5:1.

60. Grudem, *Making Sense of Man and Sin*, 39.

61. Kilner, "Humanity in God's Image," 617.

that humans should not curse other humans because they are "made in the image of God." However, it is equally clear that only Jesus Christ is called "the image of the invisible God," and those who follow Christ are being transformed into his image, through the Spirit of the Lord.[62] Only Adam, Eve, and Jesus were, at any time, perfect as humans. In order for any other human to be perfectly in the image of God, each person must "put on the new self, which is being renewed in knowledge after the image of its creator."[63] Therefore, although every human being participates in the image of God simply because he or she is human, humans more fully participate in the *imago Dei*, or what it essentially means to be human, to the extent that they submit themselves to God. Scripture affirms that God's laws were given for the good of humanity.[64] To refuse to submit to the commands of God is to participate in sin and to fight against the original purposes for humanity. For example, when a man and a woman produce children, the children are made in the image of their parents. However, although those children continue to image their parents even if they rebel against everything they are taught, they participate better in the image of their parents if they imitate their parents' character. The Bible relays this same idea when it exhorts believers to "be imitators of God, as dearly beloved children."[65]

Sin is more than dastardly acts. Sin is not defined by how humans feel about things, but sin is defined by God in how a person relates to God, other humans, and also things. Grudem defines sin as "any failure to conform to the moral law of God in act, attitude, or nature."[66] Therefore, sin is primarily against God and secondarily against other people. The Ten Commandments presents, in a bare-bones sense, the moral law of God.[67] Put positively, Jesus' reduction of the law of God to loving God with one's affections as well as actions and showing others the same care one would show for himself or herself rightly displays God's will for humans.[68] Only when a person loves God with all his or her spiritual, mental, and physical strength can he or she truly love his or her fellow human being as himself or herself.

62. Colossians 1:15; 2 Corinthians 4:4; 2 Corinthians 3:18.
63. Colossians 3:10.
64. Deuteronomy 10:13.
65. Ephesians 5:1.
66. Grudem, *Making Sense of Man and Sin*," 82.
67. Exodus 20:1–7; Deuteronomy 5:6–21.
68. Matthew 22:35–40.

God created a perfect world where there was no sin, suffering, and death. However, when sin entered the world, it was accompanied by suffering and death.[69] The Bible states in many places that to follow the sinful imaginations of the human heart will result in disaster.[70] If humans are to properly reflect the image of God, they must attune their lives and communities to God's stated foundations for life. When this is not done, chaos ensues rather than the world of order that God created.

Americans of African Descent and the Image of God

American society as a whole has become a post-Christian, secular society.[71] People no longer look to God for their definition of humanness. The fact that the illegitimacy rate in the black community is over 70 percent, in conjunction with the fact that young black males are the highest perpetrators of violent crime, show that something is drastically wrong. Americans of African descent must realize that they, along with all other humans, are made in God's image. This carries a certain dignity that should be manifested by how they view themselves and live. As mentioned earlier, to be made in the image of God means that humans have a greater resemblance to God than any other creature and that humans should live in conformity to the creation mandate. However, partly because of a negative self-image and an ignorance of history, many Americans of African descent engage in self-deprecating behavior. For one to realize that he or she is made in the image of God, one must submit himself or herself to living according to the creation mandate in conjunction with God's biblical plan. Until these biblical foundations are rebuilt in the black community, the depravity experienced will remain.

If Americans of African descent recognize that they are made in the image of God and choose to live in accordance with the creation mandate under the authority of God, they will be successful in American society. The bulk of those who do well in American society continue to practice Murray's founding virtues by staying married, practicing a strong work ethic, remaining honest in their dealings, and maintaining at least a modicum of religiosity. Murray's critique of what he calls "the new upper class" is that while they tend to cling to these virtues as a base for their success, they tend

69. Genesis 2:16–17; Romans 5:12.
70. Deuteronomy 12:28; Psalm 33:12; John 3:36; Romans 2:6–11.
71. Sproul, *Lifeviews*, 21.

not to want to be judgmental toward other groups.[72] Hence, they encourage other groups to hold to ideologies that do not actually work in practice. As detailed earlier, Americans of African descent are at the bottom percentiles in all those areas among all major racial groups. If Americans of African descent want their communities to prosper, it is important to socialize their children in families and communities that hold these four virtues high.

The Biblical Idea of Authority and Human Community

Most children are born into community. They are conceived by a male parent and a female parent; they are raised by at least one of those parents; those households in which the children are raised exists within some type of community; that community exists within a city, a state, and a country on Earth. Within each of those structures exists some type of governmental system. Families are usually governed by at least one parent, and countries are governed by a president, a director, a group, some type of separation of powers, or a king/dictator. However, in order for each system to work properly, whether governmental, family, or business, that system needs some type of government or leadership. It is government's duty to protect people from all forms of evil by bringing justice to all and maintaining order. Government should work for what is best for its people and serve them.[73] Government was created to add structure and leadership to human communities. Government was not created so the people could serve a certain group or a person.[74]

The two main passages in the New Testament that detail the duties of government and how people should respond to it are Romans 13:1–7[75]

72. Murray, *Coming Apart*, 289–90.

73. Grudem, *Politics According to the Bible*, 78–79, 82.

74. Schaeffer, *Christian Manifesto*, 99–102.

75. Let every person be subject to the governing authorities. For there is no authority except from God, and those that exist have been instituted by God. 2 Therefore whoever resists the authorities resists what God has appointed, and those who resist will incur judgment. 3 For rulers are not a terror to good conduct, but to bad. Would you have no fear of the one who is in authority? Then do what is good, and you will receive his approval, 4 for he is God's servant for your good. But if you do wrong, be afraid, for he does not bear the sword in vain. For he is the servant of God, an avenger who carries out God's wrath on the wrongdoer. 5 Therefore one must be in subjection, not only to avoid God's wrath but also for the sake of conscience. 6 For because of this you also pay taxes, for the authorities are ministers of God, attending to this very thing. 7 Pay to all what is owed to them: taxes to whom taxes are owed, revenue to whom revenue is owed, respect

and 1 Peter 2:13–14.[76] These duties of government are delineated by Wayne Grudem in his book *Politics According to the Bible*.[77] Romans 13:1–4 manifests the duties of government. First, verses 1–2 plainly state that governmental authority has its origin in God. Although the context is speaking specifically about governmental authority, this can also be said for all authoritative positions (family, business, community, etc.). To buck against authority, as long as that authority is not promoting disobedience to God, is to buck against God. Second, the first part of verse 3 testifies that governmental rulers have the duty to punish corrupt behavior. Hence, the threat and enforcement of punishment by governmental officials are necessary to maintain a peaceful society. Third, the second part of verse 3 proclaims that good government should commend those who are doers of good. Thus, government should play a part in encouraging and commending good behavior and actions that lead to the good of society as a whole. Fourth, verse 4 teaches that those who serve in government are supposed to ultimately serve God and his good purposes. Part of this service of God is to inflict wrath on those who do wrong. Therefore, the fifth duty of government can be found in the second part of verse 4. Those who do wrong should fear the power of the government because it is government's job to avenge the rights of the innocent upon the guilty. Hence, they are to be agents of justice.

The responsibilities of citizens are found in Romans 13:5–7 and 1 Peter 2:13–14. Peter directs humans to "be subject for the Lord's sake to every human institution" in verse 13. Paul says the same in Romans 13:5 but adds that humans should not only be subject to avoid retribution but also "for the sake of conscience." Hence, God bears witness to the human conscience that submitting to authority is the correct thing to do. A second duty that citizens have, to which Romans 13:6 affirms, is to pay taxes. Since governmental officials are servants of God, they should have the proper financial support so they can effectively do their jobs. Romans 13:7 ends with exhorting citizens to give what is "owed" to government: proper "taxes," "revenue," "respect," and "honor."

All these are necessary for the good of society as a whole. Without governmental authority working for the good of all, there would be chaos.

---

to whom respect is owed, honor to whom honor is owed.

76. Be subject for the Lord's sake to every human institution, whether it be to the emperor as supreme, or to governors as sent by him to punish those who do evil and to praise those who do good.

77. Grudem, *Politics According to the Bible*, 80–82.

Now, how does one decide what is good for all? Since governmental officials are servants of God to maintain and promote the good, what is good
has to be defined as that which is good in accordance with God's purpose
of humanness. The founders of the United States wrote in the Declaration
of Independence that some truths are "self-evident." Included in these self-
evident truths are "that all men are created equal, that they are endowed
by their Creator with certain unalienable rights, that among these are life,
liberty, and the pursuit of happiness." The Declaration further states that
these rights are to be secured by government and that government shall
"derive their just powers by the consent of the governed."[78] Therefore, since
humans live in community with other humans, governmental authority is
needed for the good of the whole. It is each person and group's duty to
submit to just government. The only time that it is the duty of a citizen
to resist government is when government or laws are created that would
cause the citizen to disobey God.[79] The Apostles Peter and John invoked
this privilege in Acts 5:29 when they told their governing body that they
would not cease to preach and teach in the name of Jesus because "We
must obey God rather than men." God's commands are higher than any
human law; hence, any law that is put in place by humans must be made in
accordance with the boundaries that God's law maintains. The Declaration
of Independence concurs with this by stating "that whenever any form of
government becomes destructive of these ends (the ones quoted above in
the Declaration), it is the right of the people to alter or abolish it."

It seems to be fashionable for some Americans of African descent to
defy all authority in their lives, but that is a sure recipe for disaster. Although
most blacks are not impoverished and economically depressed, many still
ascribe to the victim mentality. As mentioned earlier, intellectuals are accepting without question that unequal outcomes are tantamount to some
type of discrimination, and they, in turn, are passing this perception on
to the populace. Thus, a type of therapeutic alienation or ressentiment is
fostered, where this supposed inequality becomes a fundamental element
in the identity of blackness.[80] Hence, due to these attitudes, many Americans of African descent, and especially American of African descent males,
may develop attitudes and practices that go contrary to mainline society. In

78. Jefferson, "Declaration of Independence."

79. Grudem, *Politics According to the Bible*, 88.

80. See chapter 2 of this book where "therapeutic alienation" and "ressentiment" are
discussed.

an attempt to resist being white, many Americans of African descent have created their own brand of blackness that is often openly defiant against mainstream society. This defiance is an attempt to attain power in society. Therefore, many Americans of African descent show disdain for traditional forms of authority, to their own hurt.

Clyde Franklin II argued that American of African descent males seem to experience deteriorated standards of social behavior due to their appropriation from Africa, subhuman treatment in America, and subsequent exclusion from American mainstream masculinity.[81] As a result, many tend to feel as though their situations are hopeless. While this may have been true of those earlier generations through the end of Jim Crow, the later generations who know nothing of that diminished masculinity are still displaying a lack of ascendency. Americans of African descent are present in all levels of American society, and there is no legal impediment that prohibits any person from being anything he or she wants to be. This seems to prove a type of socialization into this way of thinking even when the external barriers have been removed. Although Franklin's perceived reasons for the problems are no longer valid, the problems still exist.

Franklin proposes five ways black men respond to this anomie in attempts to gain power or success in American society. Franklin's first group is called "conforming black masculinity." These are those who wholeheartedly conform to the morals and values of manhood in the dominant culture. Those in the second group, those who can be identified with "ritualistic black masculinity," go with the flow similar to the first group, but there is no real buy-in, hence their actions become "ritualistic." "Innovative black masculinity" is the third group. Franklin suggests that this group is "the most publicized, feared, and reviled black man in America today." The innovators create an alternative masculinity. Franklin placed the gangster rappers, the drug dealers, and the delinquents in this group. The fourth group is described as "retreatist black masculinity." Those in this group practice a type of drop out masculinity because they are jobless, homeless, drug and/or alcohol dependent, and underachievers. The final group is "rebellious black masculinity." Franklin asserts that black men rarely fall within this group. To fall within this group, one must reject both American ideals and the avenues of reaching those ideals. Usually, black men may refuse to ascribe to one or the other but rarely both.[82]

81. Franklin, "Ain't I a Man?," 275–77.
82. Franklin, "Ain't I a Man?," 280–82.

As Franklin said, the predominant form of masculinity that is being pushed today as the true model for blackness is "innovative black masculinity." Since they feel that they do not fit in with mainstream society, many Americans of African descent have chosen to celebrate defiance. The disrespect for authority shown by many Americans of African descent is an attempt to gain power. Abby Peterson refers to this attitude as the "code of the streets." In other words, young people try to gain a type of respect by exerting their independence from traditional authority figures.[83] Since those who follow the code on the streets have rejected the self-esteem that is built by acceptance of and success in mainstream culture, the type of respect that a person seeks in this case is that which is given by his or her peers. As well, those who hold to the code of the street may become exceedingly defensive and even more defiant when mainstream society rejects their values as aberrant. People can either show respect or disdain by their use of body language or other actions.[84] The innovative form of black masculinity actively fights against conformity with mainstream society.

As mentioned earlier, for any subgroup of American culture to be successful in American society, it must submit to the basic cultural norms of standard language and business culture. The only way to avoid this and still ascribe to innovative black masculinity is by rising above the culture, like many professional athletes, musicians, and celebrities have done, or to change the culture. Those with great wealth (professional athletes, musicians, and celebrities) can live above mainstream culture because their money and fame allow them to do that. However, most people cannot do that because they do not have the means. The idea that one does not have to live by the rules that govern American society has hurt many Americans of African descent. Everyone wants a hero. Unfortunately, the heroes and role models for many children of Americans of African descent are professional athletes or rap artists who glamorize criminal behavior.[85] The culture is changing and becoming more accepting of varying conducts of dress, speech, family life, and sexual preferences. However, it does not mean that those various modes of living will produce the desired result (the good life) just because society is more accepting of them. When people live outside of God's intention for them, the end product is usually chaos, to some extent or another.

83. Peterson, "Who 'Owns' the Streets?," 99–100.
84. Peterson, "Who 'Owns' the Streets?," 100.
85. Williams, *Enough*, 90.

Although it sounds almost negative, most Americans of African descent who do well for themselves in mainstream society ascribe to what Franklin called "conforming black masculinity." Conformists do not reject the ideals that made America great, they heartily accept them. Those values have no color attached to them. Frederick Douglass said it plainly, "My theory of self-made men is, then, simply this; they are men of work."[86] Bell Hooks explained that many black men exchange "a work ethic based on integrity and ethical values" for a success model of making money even if it means "lying and cheating."[87] Juan Williams proposed a four-step plan for the next generation to stay out of poverty. The first step is to at least complete high school, although completing college would be even better. Next, it is important to get a career job. The intention of longevity in the profession is an important part of this step. After that, one should marry, but only after completing one's education and after obtaining a job. The final step is to only have children after the age of twenty-one and while one is married.[88] It could be added that unless one learns to submit to the authority figures in one's life, he or she will never be productive in society. Anthony B. Bradley proposed that if Americans of African descent focused on "freedom, responsibility, and dignity" rather than "self-sabotaging behavior," the result would be increased education, less criminality, and higher marriage rates.[89] The bottom line is this; there is no magic pill. If Americans of African descent are to get on par with other American groups, they will have to accept that they are a part of the larger American fabric and work hard to give themselves and their children a future. As well, they need to begin to socialize their children into a culture where marriage longevity, family, education, and a good value system are the main foci.

Not a White or a Black Thing, but a Human Thing

The Bible declares that all human beings are sinners. Romans 3:23 boldly declares, "For all have sinned and fall short of the glory of God." Every race, creed, and people group is dominated by sin. The Bible further states in Romans 3:10–12, "None is righteous, no, not one; no one understands; no one seeks for God . . . no one does good, not even one." When the Bible speaks

86. Douglass, "Self-Made Men," 138.
87. Hooks, *We Real Cool*, 18.
88. Williams, *Enough*, 215.
89. Bradley, *Black and Tired*, 2.

of the depravity of all human beings, it neither means that people have no understanding of what is wrong or right, nor does it mean that people are as bad as imaginable. Many human beings do things that seem honorable and good. However, human depravity does mean that every human being, even from birth, has a powerful proclivity toward sin, especially in regards to motives, and that he or she is utterly powerless without the help of God to disengage himself or herself from his or her depravity.[90]

That being said, if any human being chooses to point out another's sins, he or she should do so with humility. As mentioned earlier, the practice of slavery was ubiquitous in the ancient world. Was it still wrong? Of course it was. The understanding of the dignity of human beings demands that any subjugation of any human being below others is wrong, whether a person consents to that subjugation or not. Both the biblical doctrine that declares that all human beings are made in the image of God and the American Declaration of Independence agree that all humans, regardless of race, gender, or financial bracket, share equality in regards to their humanness. Thus, no human being is inherently inferior to any other. However, being sinful, human beings and human groups will often take advantage of weaker human beings, and history all too often proves this truth.

What can be done about the debt owed by America to Americans of African descent for all the years of slavery and Jim Crow? Americans partially paid with the blood of her sons through the bloodiest war Americans ever fought, the Civil War.[91] Later, Americans tried to make things right in regards to Jim Crow by passing laws to make all discrimination illegal.[92] Although it took many years to get here, there is absolutely no legal reason today that any person of any race cannot be anything he or she desires. Americans of African descent are serving or have served in just about all areas of government, business, and entertainment. Are people still prejudiced? Of course they are. People of all races, including Americans of African descent, are still prejudiced because humans are sinful. But it is now illegal to allow discriminatory practices to be applied to public venues. Hence, the chains in their own minds are the only obstacles holding Americans of African descent back today.

90. Erickson, *Christian Theology*, 627–31.

91. Cornelison and Yanak, *Great American History Fact-Finder*, 100. About 620,000 lost their lives due to the Civil War; this is almost as much as the loss of life in all other American wars combined.

92. Cornelison and Yanak, *Great American History Fact-Finder*, 269.

None of the Americans who held slaves are alive today. The people of the last generation that saw and understood Jim Crow laws are growing old and diminishing. Times have changed greatly since those days. The Christian response to the debt is to forgive, especially when something has been done to try to rectify the issue. Mark 11:25 says, "And whenever you stand praying, forgive, if you have anything against anyone, so that your Father also who is in heaven may forgive you your trespasses." The little word translated "in order that" begins a *hina* (ἵνα) clause, which expresses either purpose or result.[93] Hence, the passage is saying that those who desire for God to forgive them for their sins should not withhold forgiveness from others. All humans are sinful, thus one should not be so prideful to refuse forgiveness to others, because we all need it from God. After offering forgiveness, Americans of African descent must choose to rebuild. The greatest step in their rebuilding process will be discussed in the next chapter.

All humans are made in the image of God. This sets humans apart from every other creature. Ephesians 5:1 exhorts humans to "be imitators of God, as dearly beloved children." Since humans are made in the image of God, they are to fulfil the cultural mandate under God's authority and as God's earthly royal stewards. Furthermore, living in community with other humans means living under authority. Authority is a creation of God to make for an orderly society. Without it, there can only be chaos. Americans of African descent should recognize that they are very valuable; they are created in God's image. However, they must also recognize that they live in community with all other Americans. America is just as much their country as anyone else's. Therefore, the tried and true methods that made other ordinary Americans successful will also work for them. There will always be those on the fringe who choose to remain in the past. But all Americans with an eye toward the future must join arms and work together to restore God's original plan for humanity.

In the next chapter, the ideal of how communities of Americans of African descent can be salvaged will be presented. It is understood that the ideal is not always possible, but unless one is given a target at which to aim, it is very likely that he or she will never hit it, or even come close. God Almighty gave humans a better way to live. Those who fail to take heed do so to their own peril.

---

93. Dana and Mantey, *Manual Grammar of the Greek New Testament*, 283, 286.

Chapter 4

A New Value System
Biblical Family Formation

There are only two ways a person can recover what has been lost. A person can either find the exact thing that was lost, or he or she can try to rebuild what was lost by redoing exactly what was done to make the first one. What was lost in the black community is not a thing that can be recovered. History is time past. However, what was lost in communities of Americans of African descent can be rebuilt. Most so-called solutions to the problems in the black community seek to add to the community by putting programs in place that will address the fruit or the specific issues (teenage pregnancy, failure to complete high school, single woman-headed households, juvenile delinquency, and adult male unemployment)[1] rather than address the root of those issues. When Jesus addressed the church at Ephesus about losing "the love you had at first," he did not tell them to go to a self-help seminar to learn how to love or add a bunch of programs that would treat the symptoms of that lack of love. He told them to "remember therefore from where you have fallen, repent, and do the works you did at first."[2] In essence, this was an authoritative order to turn from what they were doing wrong (clear the slab) and rebuild using the original blueprints. This is a good starting point for any rebuilding project. If a person loses his or her house due to fire or some other catastrophe, he or she can never

---

1. Majors, "Conclusion and Recommendations," 305.
2. Revelation 2:4–5.

regain the same house. However, the same house can be rebuilt if they clear the slab and the diagram that was used to build the first house is also used to rebuild the second.

To "remember therefore from where you have fallen" means to think back to the time when the right foundations were in place; think back to the time before things began veering off course. Since the word "remember" (μνημόνευε) is the first word in Revelation 2:5, it is emphatic. The word is present tense, meaning that one should continually remember, and in the imperative mood, connoting a command. The fact that they had "fallen" means that they were not where they were at first. "You have fallen" (πέπτωκας) is perfect tense, which implies that the falling of those in the Ephesian church began in the past and continued during the time of the writing. The second and third actions in this verse, to "repent" (μετανόησον) and to "do" (ποίησον), are both aorist in action and imperative in mood. This expresses that the participants at the church of Ephesus were commanded both to turn from the direction that was wrong and to redo what was done when the right foundations were in place, and they were to do so decisively.[3]

This chapter will deal with those foundations and how to redo those works that were done at first. There was only one time in history when human beings were headed in the right direction, and that is when God created the first man and woman. Although humans can never attain that level of perfection while in these sinful bodies, that should still be humanity's goal. When Jesus was asked by a group of religious leaders if "it was lawful to divorce one's wife for any cause," Jesus did not refer to reasons for the divorce, hardships in the relationship, or contemporary theories of marriage and family. He referred back to God's original intention for humanity. He said that God "made them male and female," and marriage entails that "a man shall leave his father and his mother and hold fast to his wife and the two shall become one flesh." Thus, the answer to their question was, "what therefore God has joined together let not man separate."[4] God's original intention for humanity is the standard by which one should judge what is best for humans to pursue and how humans should live. In order for any person or community to live in harmony with authentic humanity, which is the authentic image of God, he or she must strive to live according to God's original intention for humanity. This chapter will explore a possible

3. Kistemaker, *Revelation*, 120.
4. Matthew 19:3–6.

solution to the problems experienced by Americans of African descent by revisiting God's original intention for humanity.

God's Order: A Familial Foundation

As established in chapter 1, Americans of African descent, as a group, suffer more in the areas of economics, education, traditional family development, and socialization than any other major racial group in America. In chapter 2, it was proven that the source of that lack of development has less to do with factors outside the group and more to do with norms and practices accepted by the group. Chapter 3 demonstrated that while all humans share in the dignity of the image of God and thus possess inherent value above the remainder of creation, all humans are still sinful and will therefore do injury to themselves as well as to others if left to themselves. Since all humans are created in God's image and descended from a single pair, it would be reasonable to assume that if any one group is suffering pathologies more than others, something happened along the way to aid in the development of those pathologies. It is the intention of this book to prove that the missing element in many families of Americans of African descent is a biblically-based family support system.

If each group descended from a single pair as the Bible affirms, then whatever developed within the various races was either passed down through genetic pairing, by communal socialization, or a combination of both. Even Herrnstein and Murray admit that intelligence is partially shaped by the environment.[5] Inherited genes do affect people. However, the environment in which a person is socialized also matters. When a child's parents divorce or when a child is reared in a dysfunctional home, both behavior and school performance are usually affected, regardless of genes.[6] Hence, humans are not destined to a certain fate because of their pedigree; they can choose to make a better future for themselves if they are willing to put proper disciplines in place. Although Lawrence Steinburg agrees that genetics affect child intelligence, he also argues that environmental factors, like "extreme trauma," "violence inside and outside the home," and "the chronic distress associated with poverty," may better explain "the relative intellectual deficiencies of children from poorer families."[7]

5. Herrnstein and Murray, *Bell Curve*, 390.
6. Bond, "Secrets of Success," 1, 3.
7. Steinberg, *Age of Opportunity*, 165.

When God created humans, the first institution he put in place was a social institution: the family. In the expanded explanation of the creation of humans in Genesis 2, God joined the man and the woman together as "one flesh" (Gen 2:24) or what C. S. Lewis referred to as "a single organism."[8] Lewis went on to say that in similar fashion to likening "a lock and its key" or "a violin and its bow" as "one organism," so are a husband and a wife.[9] In other words, as the foundation of a family, the one is incomplete without the other; together they lay the proper foundation for the family. In the overview of the creation of humans in Genesis 1 in the first part of the cultural mandate, God commanded humans to "be fruitful and multiply" (Gen 1:28). This means that they were to socialize new generations within families. God's directive to humans to bear children was an injunction "to cover the earth with God's glorious image and likeness."[10]

This social institution of the family was to be the primary source for the socialization of education, norms, and values of the individual. The family is, for most people, the very first means—as well as the primary method—of assimilation into human culture. This socialization helps to develop how people view the world and is a major facilitator of core convictions, values, morals, and customs. Hence, family socialization helps to create a person's foundation for how he or she will live. It provides a ground for how a person understands gender roles, how a person communicates, how a person views and responds to authority figures, what a person sees as good or bad, beautiful or unsavory, and how a person should respond to conflicts or difficulties, and also adds a template for how people should respond to interpersonal relations.[11] These things are both taught and caught through family socialization.

However, what is being taught and caught through many families of Americans of African descent is drastically different from the original model God founded. In families where proper male role models are absent, the ideas of what a good man should be as a prospective mate for females and a proper model of manhood for boys are often skewed. As well, when fathers and husbands are lacking, mothers have to adapt to cover the essential duties of both roles. Hence, many American of African descent boys

8. Lewis, *Mere Christianity*, 104.

9. Lewis, *Mere Christianity*, 104.

10. Schrock, "Equipping the Generations," 62–63.

11. Moore, Ford, and Milner, "Underachievement among Gifted Students of Color," 169.

tend to see women differently than others who enjoy the benefit of seeing a mother and father engaged properly in gender roles. They tend to especially struggle with female authority figures.[12] In absence of godly fathers as role models, street life and peers reinforce an alternative masculinity of "toughness, sexual promiscuity, material possessions, and thrill-seeking."[13] This is a recipe for disaster.

The raw foundational tools for proper masculinity and femininity in males and females are normally resident within them from birth. Dwight N. Hopkins argues that although males and females are born with their respective male or female body parts, the actual gender a person possesses is a sociological process.[14] Hopkins' argument is not totally consistent with either physiological or sociological aspects of humanity. The far majority of humans tend to exhibit behaviors consistent with their anatomical sex throughout their lives. Although some aspects of maleness and femaleness are sociological, the raw stuff that makes for maleness and femaleness is hormones. In other words, not only are the physical sexual features that belong to each gender natural and God-given, but the workings in the body that make for the maleness and femaleness of the respective genders are also natural and God-given. In males, testosterone is the major hormone that makes boys become competitive little risk-takers, more masculine looking and sounding, and physically stronger than women as they grow. Even while still an embryo, testosterone begins to form the bodies of those who possess the Y chromosome into males. In females, the major hormone is estrogen, which makes them more womanly.[15]

Nevertheless, these masculine and feminine roles still need proper socialization models to develop in a manner that properly displays the image of God. Without fathers in the home, boys and girls tend to gravitate towards aberrancy. The same testosterone that drives boys to be stronger and more competitive is the same hormone that can drive them to crime, violence, and other deviant behaviors if not controlled. It is a well-known fact that males are involved in more criminal behavior than females,[16] and this is greatly due to uncontrolled testosterone. Although men tend to have "ten to twenty times" the testosterone as women, men and women who are

12. Majors, "Conclusion and Recommendations," 310.
13. Majors, "Conclusion and Recommendations," 312–13.
14. Hopkins, "New Black Heterosexual Male," 215–16.
15. Dobson, *Bringing Up Boys*, 19–23.
16. Wagner, "United States Incarceration Rates by Sex, 2010."

involved in more aggressive professions or activities tend to have higher levels of testosterone, in respect to their genders.[17] In the same way that fire can be used constructively or destructively, so this inward combustible power can be directed for either good or bad. Many children gravitate toward bad behavior during their teenage years, but children who go over the edge usually lack a loving relationship with a parent at home who can help deter that self-destructive behavior.[18] If for nothing else, a father, due to his physical strength, booming voice, and more intimidating demeanor, has greater success disciplining children, especially in the teen years. As well, it is commonly believed by many psychologists that a girl's future associations with the opposite sex are either positively or negatively influenced by how she related to her father in her youth.[19]

Lawrence Steinburg testified that the adolescent proclivity toward risk-taking is ubiquitous in all nations and cultures.[20] Hence, not just American-born youths, of all races, share this proclivity, but also youths born in every other part of the world. Steinburg further declared that "adolescents take more risks than either children or adults, and the incidence of risky behavior usually peaks somewhere during the late teens. Violence peaks at this age. So do self-inflicted injuries, unintentional drownings, experimentation with drugs, accidental pregnancies, property crime, and fatal automobile crashes."[21] Why are adolescents more likely to do these things? Although adolescents seem to reason as well as adults when under no stress, the adolescent's prefrontal cortex, which among other things regulates impulse control, is not fully developed until about the mid-twenties. Hence, the thrill- and reward-seeking drives in youths are more difficult to control, and therefore, without the proper environment, they could get into a lot of trouble. This is why it is of utmost importance that the environment in which children are reared is one that is both loving and controlled.[22] God, in his infinite wisdom, designed that children should be brought up during this most sensitive of times, i.e., adolescence, through the guidance and discipline of parents who can guide their development and decisions.

17. Wagner, "United States Incarceration Rates by Sex, 2010," 21–23.

18. Wagner, "United States Incarceration Rates by Sex, 2010," 42.

19. Dobson, *Complete Marriage and Family Home Reference Guide*, 237–38.

20. Steinberg, *Age of Opportunity*, 84.

21. Steinberg, *Age of Opportunity*, 68–69.

22. Steinberg, *Age of Opportunity*, 70–77, 84.

It is not simply a mother and a father being present that create good families but mothers and fathers building strong relationships with their children and modeling good behavior that make for productive God-fearing children. Before the present information age where children are now being bombarded with various philosophical voices, character building seemed to be less challenging. However, in this modern time, parents have to compete for the souls of their children against the philosophies of secular media, the philosophies of rap artists, and the philosophies of a secular educational system, all of which belong to a world that rejects the moral teachings of Scripture.[23] When children experience a family modeled within the confines of a loving, reaffirming, and disciplined environment, they often will make good choices because they see the benefit of moral rules, and they do not want to disappoint their parents.[24] Building family traditions, sharing regular family outings, and dealing with problems in an affirming and conversational atmosphere are important bonds that need to be nurtured from the earliest of ages.[25] Simple things like eating together at least once a day or watching family movies with popcorn and/or other snacks go a long way in constructing family closeness. A home should be a safe place where people are encouraged, through discipline, love, and un-conditional acceptance to live responsibly before God and other people.[26] It is much more difficult for defiance and rebellion to exist where each party likes the other and constructive relationships are fostered. However, it is important that parental authority, the ability to maintain boundaries and discipline, is not sacrificed on the altar of friendship.[27] Parents should never lose control of the household; yet they should never be autocratic. The Bible commands fathers to rear children "in the discipline and instruction of the Lord" without "provoking your children to anger."[28]

The Bible teaches that the education of children is to be the primary responsibility of parents, not the government.[29] As a matter of fact, the Bible holds parents responsible for all molding and training of their own children. In Deuteronomy 6:7, the Bible directs parents to teach God's

23. McIlhaney and Bush, *Girls Uncovered*, 19–21.
24. Steinburg, *Age of Opportunity*, 125–26.
25. Steinburg, *Age of Opportunity*, 131.
26. Cloud and Townsend, *Safe People*, 144.
27. Dobson, *Bringing Up Boys*, 215–17.
28. Ephesians 6:4.
29. Grudem, *Politics According to the Bible*, 247.

commands "diligently to your children, and [you] shall talk about them when you sit in your house, and when you walk by the way, and when you lie down, and when you rise." In other words, God's truth should be the foundation of all instruction for human beings, whether that instruction is part of the so-called secular disciplines of mathematics and science or the moral formation of values.[30] Although there is no biblical injunction against public education or using teachers who specialize in their respective fields, parents pay the taxes that support the educational system, and they vote in the members of the school board. The schools work for the parents, and parents should demand that schools support their values and desires.[31]

The family consisting of a biological father and a biological mother living and working together and submitting under the authority of God is the best form of human socialization. A basic fact of history is that the traditional family unit founded on a committed marriage between a man and a woman has been the cornerstone of civic human civilizations.[32] The strength and stability of families have immense value to communities because they are the fabric that binds the human race.[33] Families are made of individuals, strong communities are made of families, and communities are the building blocks of cities, states, and countries. Each family began with a contribution from a male and a female. However, maleness and femaleness means so much more than their physical contributions to human life. Not only do the different temperaments of the masculine father and the feminine mother add to the stability of the emotional development of the child, but other factors are at work for the betterment of the family as a whole.

Lisa A. Gennetian listed four ways that family dynamics affect childhood success. First, a two-parent-led family tends to make more money than a one-person-led household does, so there are more resources for the betterment of children. Just about all studies show that children reared in single mother households, as a group, will grow to be less educated, attain less financially, and have more out-of-wedlock births themselves. Second, family structure, along with its ethics and manners presented therein, is often emulated by children in their own future families. In other words, good and/or bad family practices are often perpetuated throughout the

30. Gentry, "Sermon: Raising Children, the Christian Way," 97.
31. Dobson, *Complete Marriage and Family Guide*, 128.
32. Bradley, *Black and Tired*, 12.
33. Segura-April, "Religion and the Family," 781.

generations. Third, "social control theory" puts forward the idea that various controls placed on youthful deeds produce different consequences. Hence, when social controls are absent or barely there, many children will push the limits toward degeneracy. The final way that family dynamics affect childhood success is through the "stress theory." Any disruption in the normality of the family dynamics in the child's life, including but not limited to "divorce, remarriage, relocation, or unemployment," adds stress to the child, which can negatively affect his or her behavior.[34] Children born and raised in the traditional family unit, led by the married biological father and mother of their children, show, on a whole, to do better in school, gain better incomes in adulthood, maintain better health, and are better behaved than any other family structure, including step-parent/biological-parent unions, cohabitating parental unions (even if both are biological parents), single parent, foster parents, and non-parental relatives as guardians.[35] Once again, this substantiates God's wisdom. The biological father and mother in a married, one-flesh relationship proves to be the best foundation for families.

Families and Americans of African Descent

In communities of Americans of African descent, the traditional practice of an intact marriage and family is rare. Anthony B. Bradley expressed concern over the staggering statistics that almost 43 percent of black pregnancies are terminated by abortion and, of those who are allowed to be born, over 70 percent are born out of wedlock.[36] As mentioned above, families founded on married couples, especially consisting of both biological parents, tend to be more economically stable and their children tend to be better disciplined, do better in school, and are more upwardly mobile in their adult years. Ralph Richard Banks, in his eye-opening work *Is Marriage for White People? How the African American Marriage Decline Affects Everyone*, shows that marriage is declining among Americans of African descent more than any other racial group in America.[37] Banks's research agreed with Charles

34. Gennetian, "One or Two Parents? Half or Step Siblings? The Effect of Family Structure on Young Children's Achievement," 417–18.

35. Schneider, Atteberry, and Owens, "Family Matters: Family Structure and Child Outcomes," 3, 10, 12, 14, 18, 22–24.

36. Bradley, *Black and Tired*, 22.

37. Banks, *Is Marriage for White People?*, 7–8.

Murray's findings in *Coming Apart* that proved that higher educated and higher earning people tend to marry at greater rates. However, although the higher educated and higher earning black males and females are more likely to get married than those not so upwardly mobile, they are still "twice as likely" to be single, or if they are married, "twice as likely" to get divorced as whites in the same financial bracket.[38] Many base the dearth of marriages in communities of Americans of African descent on the residual effects of slavery.[39] However, it is well-known that the marriage rates of blacks and whites in the United States were virtually the same until the 1960s.[40] If black marriages were relatively strong one hundred years after American slavery ended and during the Jim Crow era, what was the cause of the decline of marriage in communities of Americans of African descent?

Bradley concluded that "disconnecting human life, marriage, and family from their correct foundation in God is literally destroying communities and keeping generations enslaved to self-destructive behavior."[41] This is the reason marriage is declining in all racial groups in America but at an even greater pace among Americans of African descent. Robert Bork made note that both the British and American violent crime rates rose alongside the illegitimacy rates.[42] There is no wonder that young black males are the highest propagators of violent crime among all racial groups.[43] When strong adult male role models are absent from a boy's life, he depends more on his peers for support, approval, and self-image. Hence, whatever the group values, the child values, even if it is gang violence, sexual conquests, or disregard for authority. The values of many of these peer groups fail to promote those practices that will make for a successful and fulfilling adult life within the wider culture. In much of the black community, educational ascendency is often equated with being a nerd, trying to act white, or being a sissy, and is thus shunned by the group. Those who follow these self-sabotaging behaviors limit their own futures through the acquisition

38. Banks, *Is Marriage for White People?*, 8–10.
39. Patrick, "Outside Insiders," 108.
40. Hattery and Smith, "Families of Incarcerated African American Men," 138.
41. Bradley, *Black and Tired*, 23.
42. Bork, *Slouching Towards Gomorrah*, 155.
43. Gaylord-Harden, Zakaryan, Bernard, and Pekoc, "Community-Level Victimization and Aggressive Behavior in African American Male Adolescents: Profile Analysis," 503. See also McWhorter, *Losing the Race*, 13.

of prison records, low educational attainment, and poor social skills.[44] In an attempt to gain respect through this alternative manhood model, they lay a foundation that makes it much more difficult to reach the authentic manhood the Bible presents, where self-sacrificial responsible behavior is valued. Based on the fact that God gave the first human pair the creation mandate in Genesis 1:28, God's plan for human civilization was for societies to be based on strong families, and those families were to be based on strong marriages. Why is it a mystery that Americans of African descent as a group are toward the bottom in the areas of wealth, education, and socialization in society when their families are in disarray? All these things are boosted through family stability. To follow God's creative order in God's way brings peace, success, and order. To go against God's creative order brings chaos. This is what many in communities of Americans of African descent are experiencing.

Declining marriage rates in communities of Americans of African descent display a serious misunderstanding of intimacy. Americans of African descent are engaging in romantic relationships; children are still being born, or in many cases, aborted. Yet many of their relationships are not in line with what God created them to be because they are not within the confines of a committed marriage relationship. When children fail to see patterns of fidelity in long-term marriage relationships, the concept of the necessity of marriage becomes minimized in their eyes. In other words, whatever patterns of life into which a child is socialized are the patterns that the child feels are normal.[45] The family is still the main way humans attain their cultural values, religious beliefs, and socialization skills, whether that family is founded on a loving and faithful relationship between a husband and a wife, founded on a single mother, or founded within the confines of an abusive environment.[46] Many children are raised within the boundaries of a cohabiting relationship or loose sexual relationships modeled by their single parent. Cohabitation and loose sexuality devalue commitment and God's mandate against sex outside of marriage. As well, people who live together in romantic relationships outside of marriage are less likely to bring their incomes together for the good of the children and the household in

44. Harris, "Black Male Masculinity and Same Sex Friendships," 81–82, 84.

45. Murray, *Coming Apart*, 158.

46. Hood, Brevard, Nguyen, and Belgrave, "Stress Among African American Emerging Adults," 77.

general, thus poverty is much more prevalent in cohabitating homes than in homes where the man and the woman are married to each other.[47]

Sexuality and sex are no longer seen as something exclusive to the marriage relationship in contemporary society.[48] High illegitimacy rates point to a misunderstanding or a devaluing in black communities of human sexuality. Hence, it is almost normal to think that all relationships where physical attraction is involved should include sex. "Hooking up," a term used in contemporary society for physically intimate liaisons without the necessity for future romantic obligations, is common and an acceptable practice in today's culture.[49] Ralph Richard Banks reports that marital infidelity is more prevalent among Americans of African descent than any other racial group, and these extra relationships seem to reflect the same patterns of the hook-up culture.[50] However, the Bible maintains that God created marriage to be a lifelong, committed, one-flesh relationship and marriage should be the only venue for human sexual expression.

The Biblical Testimony on the Proper Usage of Sex

Sex was created by God, therefore sex is not something dirty or degrading. Sex is good when used within its intended bounds. The Bible exalts sexual expression within the confines of marriage, but strongly denounces sexual practice outside the marriage union. A good example of this is in Hebrews 13:4, where the Bible says, "Let marriage be held in honor among all, and let the marriage bed be undefiled, for God will judge the sexually immoral and the adulterous." This particular verse has three parts. It upholds that biblical marriage should be held in honor by all, sexual expression within the confines of marriage is "undefiled," and God's judgment rests upon those who exercise sexual expression outside of marriage.

First of all, marriage should be "held in honor among all." The writer of Hebrews does not consider whether the decision to honor marriage is

47. Liu and Heiland, "Should We Get Married?," 19.

48. Banks, *Is Marriage for White People?*, 20.

49. McIlhaney and Bush, *Girls Uncovered*, 29–30.

50. Banks, *Is Marriage for White People?*, 50–54. This includes cohabitating relationships, where American of African descent men are "five times as likely as their white counterparts to also be involved in a long-term relationship with another woman," as well as legally married relationships, where "black married men are twice as likely as white married men to have a relationship with another woman" (53–54).

something left to personal preference, but the force of the verse is in the imperative mood.[51] "Among all" in the original Greek is ἐν πᾶσιν. It can be translated as either masculine, which carries the understanding of "among all men," or it can be translated as neuter, which carries the meaning "in all circumstances."[52] Either way, the meaning is clear. Marriage should not be pushed aside as something inconsequential. Since God is the creator of marriage, it is honorable before God and should be held in honor by humans.

Secondly, "the marriage bed," which is obviously another way of expressing marital sexual intimacy, should be kept "undefiled." The word used for "undefiled" is ἀμίαντος. The term refers to a ceremonial holiness before God; hence, there is nothing unclean or dirty about marital sex.[53] The ways expressed here to defile the marriage bed are through sexual immorality and adultery.

Finally, those who violate the marriage union, the "sexually immoral" (πορνεία) and "adulterers" (μοιχεία), stand under the wrath and judgment of God. Although "sexual immorality" (πορνεία) is often used in the Bible in a broad sense to refer to all forms of sexual impurity, Kyle Harper brought out that the technical use of πορνεία during the first century pertained to those sexual acts, like prostitution or sex with a slave, that do not "violate female honor," while μοιχεία was a technical term used for sex acts that are a "violation of a woman's sexual honor," like adultery. Harper went on to say that the "fundamental distinction" between the two words deals with "marriageable and non-marriageable women."[54] In modern society, πορνεία would stand for casual sexual expression from hook-ups to pornography. The point of the matter is that all sexual expression outside of the marriage covenant between one man and one woman stand under God's judgment. Hence, Hebrews 13:4 commands that marriage should be honored by everybody in all circumstances, and a major way to honor marriage is by keeping it undefiled by avoiding sexual immorality and adultery.[55] This takes form by refraining from any form of sexual relations before marriage in obedience to God and in expectation of one's spouse, and also by being faithful to one's spouse after marriage.

51. Johnson, *Hebrews*, 341.
52. Morris, *Hebrews-Revelation*, 146.
53. Craddock, *Hebrews-Revelation*, 163.
54. Harper, *"Porneia,"* 366, 379, 368.
55. Johnson, *Hebrews*, 341.

The marriage relationship of which God approves is explained in the latter part of Genesis 2. In Genesis 2:22, God made the first woman from a rib he took from the first man and presented her to the man. In verse 23, the man called the woman "bone of my bones and flesh of my flesh," hence he called her "Woman, because she was taken out of Man." Verse 24 builds upon these prior two verses with, "Therefore a man shall leave his father and his mother and hold fast to his wife, and they shall become one flesh." The "therefore" in verse 24 displays that it is an effect of verses 22 and 23. Since Adam had no mother or father, it should be rightly concluded that the one-flesh relationship about which the writer of Genesis speaks refers to all future marriage relationships.[56] The phrases "bone of my bone" and "flesh of my flesh" are Hebrew ways of expressing familial bonds, and the terms for "leave" (עָזַב) "and "hold fast" (דָּבַק) were words used to express covenant (בְּרִית) relationship. The main usage of covenants in the Bible did not have to do with consanguineal relationships but was rather an agreement before God between two formally opposing parties or parties outside of, in the words of William A. Heth, "naturally occurring relationships" like father, mother, sister, or brother. Certain expectations were already built into natural relationships.[57] Therefore, marriage, as a covenant relationship in conjunction with verses 22 and 23 in sharing bone and flesh, forms a new relationship whereby the two unrelated beings become as closely related as flesh and blood. In other words, the man is to "leave" the former blood relationship with father, mother, brothers, and sisters and "hold fast" to the formerly unrelated woman to form a new familial unit in the place of the former one, and those two "shall become one flesh." As a result of this one-flesh relationship, future blood relations, in the form of sons and daughters, are to be made.[58]

In Matthew 19:6b, Jesus said in his commentary of the one-flesh relationship, "What therefore God has joined together, let not man separate." Jesus went on further to say in Matthew 19:9 that the only thing that can threaten this one-flesh union is "sexual immorality" (πορνεία).[59] Hence, it is reasonable to conclude that the one-flesh relationship that "God has joined together" is consummated and acted out in the exclusive sexual

56. Grudem, *Politics According to the Bible*, 214.

57. Heth, "Jesus on Divorce," 18.

58. Heth, "Jesus on Divorce," 17–18.

59. This is the broader use of πορνεία, where it is a blanket term for all types of sexual expression outside of marriage.

union between the husband and his wife, because any foreign violation of that union puts it in jeopardy by adding another party to that one-flesh union.[60] The author of the one-flesh relationship is God himself, and anything that attempts to come between that union, though it be any type of sexual immorality or adultery, is not only fighting against the union but against God himself. This is why sexual purity is so important to maintain. Sexual expression is reserved for the one-flesh union between a man and a woman and that alone.

Not only does eternal judgment from God come at the end of the age for those who do not repent of their sins and trust in Jesus, but making a practice of doing things outside of the will of God will bring the judgment of natural consequences by God in this present age. In Deuteronomy 10:13, Moses declares that the "commandments and statues" of God are intended "for your good." Similarly, God established governmental officials and laws "for your good."[61] Laws and those who enforce them are not put in place to serve themselves but to serve those to whom they are directed.[62] In the same way, God's laws are there to serve the common good of humans, and when they are disregarded the outcome results in human judgment. When human beings disregard the God-ordained boundaries in which the good gift of sex should be exercised, chaos ensues. Unfortunately, because of the high percentages of Americans of African descent born out of wedlock, many in their communities are suffering this chaos in the forms of poverty, high incarceration rates, low educational attainment, and an all-around absence of wealth.

William L. Kynes aptly chronicled how sex grew from being identified with marriage to what it has become today, "sex without consequences."[63] What has been called the sexual revolution in the 1960s and 1970s was partly produced by the proliferation of contraception, the legality of abortion on demand, and the availability of no-fault divorce. As well, the reason people marry now is often seen more as personal enrichment rather than societal responsibility.[64] Ralph Richard Banks relayed that when the world was mainly agricultural, people generally married to support interdepen-

---

60. Spencer, *Scripture, Hermeneutics, and Matthew's Jesus*, 376–77.

61. Romans 13:3–4 proclaims that governmental officials are put in place to reward good behavior and to punish evil behavior.

62. Grudem, *Politics According to the Bible*, 106.

63. Kynes, "Marriage Debate: A Public Theology of Marriage," 188.

64. Kynes, "Marriage Debate: A Public Theology of Marriage," 187–89.

18

dent family work and then, "through the mid-twentieth century in the United States," to acquire a housewife.[65] Banks also links the availability of abortion on demand and contraception to adding to the separation of sex from marriage.[66] Mary Eberstadt contends that when social welfare was introduced, it began competing "with the family as the dominant protector of the individual."[67] Therefore, the necessity of a man as breadwinner was minimized. In a similar way, contraception and abortion on demand gave women more power over sex, so the sudden availability of sexual partners without marriage made men more reluctant to marry.

Another major problem with premarital sex, whether random or in a cohabiting relationship, is that it heightens the likelihood of divorce if the person later marries.[68] Thus, the non-committed sex of contemporary society is fighting against and even helping to destroy the very institution that God founded to be the very building block of a healthy society, the family. Americans of African descent are especially feeling the sting associated with non-marital sex. Few people, if any, plan to live in poverty, have failed marriages, or decrease their employability because of criminal records. Most young people envision a positive future for themselves. However, as the old adage goes, choices have consequences, and many childhood dreams fail to materialize because of bad choices and the consequences those choices bring.[69]

Toward a Better Future through Value Formation

So how can Americans of African descent regain the human ideal? They, like all human relationships, must go back to God's original intention for humanity by promoting traditional family values. Michael Eric Dyson purports that the term traditional family values "is a code for a narrow view of how families work" and "ignores the widespread problems of those times, including child abuse and misogyny."[70] Yet, did not God set forth a plan for the family and should not humans strive to practice family living within the boundaries God set? Is child abuse and misogyny any less prevalent today?

65. Banks, *Is Marriage for White People?*, 20.
66. Banks, *Is Marriage for White People?*, 19.
67. Eberstadt, *How the West Really Lost God*, 16.
68. McIlhaney and Bush, *Girls Uncovered*, 15, 70.
69. Banks, *Is Marriage for White People?*, 15.
70. Dyson, *Between God and Gangsta Rap*, 183.

Child abuse is much more prevalent in households where the biological mother and father are not present and married to one another. According to some studies, households led by a single parent alone or with a live-in companion "were 10 times more likely to experience abuse and 8 times more likely to experience neglect."[71] Americans of African descent can no longer ignore that which God set in place to be the normal foundation of the family and expect to gain success. Until they recognize that there is a normal pattern to families and strive for that normal pattern first, they will never attain that which maximizes human flourishing in God's image. There is a form of family that is best, and that family pattern was laid in Genesis chapters 1 and 2. That family is built upon the foundation of a monogamous, lifelong relationship between the biological mother and father who together raises their children in the fear of God and submission to his will.

So how can Americans of African descent regain the human ideal? As stated in the introduction of this chapter, a good start is to follow the outline that Jesus gave the Ephesian church in Revelation 2:5a to recover their first love that they had lost. He told them, "Remember therefore from where you have fallen; repent, and do the works you did at first." It has already been established that God laid an ideal plan in Genesis 2:23–24 according to which families should be founded: the one-flesh relationship between the husband and the wife. Anything else comes in second, at best. Hence, it is important to "remember" the ideal. What must be done next is to "repent, and do the works you did at first." In other words, each person, couple, family, and group in communities of Americans of African descent must stop following human philosophies on marriage and family and work toward that ideal, if possible, or as much as possible.

The first step that communities of Americans of African descent should take is to hold up the biblical standard of marriage and the family as normative. Because humans are sinful beings, it is not always possible to attain the standard, but the biblical standard must be held up as normative, and future generations should be taught that it is normative. Many people today have little understanding of the degenerating effects of sin on human community and how sinful practices continue to have a great effect on the human race. They therefore tend to think that the way things are today are the way things are supposed to be and often oppose any effort to make

---

71. Zuckerman and Pedersen, "Child Abuse and Father Figures."

things better.[72] In this world, where a major philosophy is relativism, it is often politically incorrect to say that one family model is better than others. However, not only does the Bible support the fact that the traditional family is best, empirical evidence also supports the traditional intact family as the family model that best supports human flourishing.[73] Research clearly and convincingly manifests that children from traditional intact families possess "an educational and social" advantage over all other types of households.[74] Even though the majority of American of African descent family units differ from the ideal model, it is still important to drill into American of African descent children's minds that the traditional model is normal and create a positive expectation for them to reach for that model. What is wrong with telling men, women, boys, and girls to keep their promises to God and one another and to be faithful to one another for the rest of their lives, regardless of changing feelings? What is wrong with telling men, women, boys, and girls to care about future generations by delaying sexual gratification for marriage, and then, after marriage, to remain with their families to see them through life's difficulties? This used to be seen as honorable. How has abandoning responsibility in search of personal, selfish happiness now become a virtue?[75] When possible, fathers ought to remain faithful to their families and raise their own children as a deposit in the future. It is a well-known fact that, on a whole, married men do better financially than unmarried men.[76] In addition, some sociologists believe that men actually do better after getting married because marriage has a civilizing effect on men by forcing them to act responsibly.[77]

The next step that communities of African descent should do is to be diligent to educate their children according to a Christian worldview. As mentioned above, the Bible makes parents responsible for the training of their children.[78] Education in the Bible is never broken up into secular and religious. Whatever was taught, whether science, mathematics, or moral education, was to be passed on through the all-encompassing paradigm

---

72. Grudem, *Politics According to the Bible*, 322.

73. Liu and Heiland, "Should We Get Married?," 19.

74. Schneider, Atteberry, and Owens, "Family Matters," 1.

75. Dobson, *Bringing Up Boys*, 54.

76. Murray, *Coming Apart*, 181.

77. Murray, *Coming Apart*, 181–82.

78. Grudem, *Politics According to the Bible*, 245–47. See also Deuteronomy 6:4–7; Proverbs 1:8; 4:1; 6:20; 13:1; 23:22; 31:1; Ephesians 6:1–4.

of a biblical worldview.[79] This does not mean that all children have to be home schooled in order for parents to follow the biblical pattern, but it does mean that parents should be diligent to hold schools accountable to represent their concerns. Parental involvement is necessary to produce quality schools.[80] It is a shame that children of Americans of African descent usually graduate on what equates to an eighth grade level, a full four years academically behind white and Asian children.[81] It is important for parents to take an active role in both the religious and secular education of their children. Structure and a loving but disciplined atmosphere, especially in the elementary grades, should be emphasized both at school and in the home environment. Only through this will children be given the greatest opportunity for success as they interact in American society.[82]

If the mental programming of a secular worldview is to be resisted, intentional reprogramming is necessary. In Romans 12:2, the Bible says, "Do not be conformed to this world, but be transformed by the renewal of your mind, that by testing you may discern what is the will of God, what is good and acceptable and perfect." The two verbs for "do not be conformed" and "be transformed" are both imperative in mood, which means that they are not optional for Christians; passive in voice, which means that something is acting upon the subject; and present in tense, which means that the action is continual or habitual. The fact that Paul, the writer of Romans, is commanding his readers not to be conformed to the world's way of doing things but to be transformed from it means that humans can either resist or cooperate with these actions. The word for "do not be conformed" is συσχηματίζεσθαι and speaks of behavior that is "formed," "molded," or "patterned."[83] Its root word is σχῆμα, which suggests that the influence to conform comes from outside rather than inwardly. The word σχῆμα represents "scheme" in English. The thing that Christians should not allow themselves to be conformed to is "this world." The phrase τῷ αἰῶνι τούτῳ "to this world" is literally "to this age" and denotes not the physical world, but the system of this world that is characterized by sinful human philosophies and actions in opposition to God. However, Christians should allow themselves to be transformed. The word for "be transformed"

79. Gentry, "Sermon: Raising Children, the Christian Way," 97–98.

80. Dobson, *Complete Marriage and Family Home Reference Guide*, 128.

81. Grudem, *Politics According to the Bible*, 253–54.

82. Dobson, *Complete Marriage and Family Home Reference Guide*, 126–27.

83. Louw and Nida, "Do Not Be Conformed. . .," 507.

is μεταμορφοῦσθαι and denotes a change of "the essential form or nature."[84] Its root word is μορφή, which denotes inward change. This word is represented by the English word "metamorphosis," where, like the change of a caterpillar into a butterfly, a complete change that begins inwardly is envisioned. The metamorphosis takes place through "the renewal of your mind" (τῇ ἀνακαινώσει τοῦ νοός). Hence, as earlier emphasized through the use of μορφή, the action works its way through the individual from an inward work of the Holy Spirit applying the word of God. The end result of the metamorphosis through renewing the mind is "that by testing you may discern what is the will of God." The word δοκιμάζειν, or "to test," means "to put to the test for the purpose of approving." Hence, after a person stops allowing himself or herself to be conformed to the pattern of this sinful age, but allows himself or herself to be metamorphosed by renewing his or her mind, only then can he or she recognize and accept God's will, because it is "good and acceptable and perfect."[85]

Therefore, to resist being shaped into the mold of this age so that one's thinking can be thoroughly changed inwardly to be able to receive God's original plan for humans will take intentionally allowing oneself to be put in the position where God can make a change that begins in one's heart. This is not easy, because the spirit and philosophies of this age are continually trying to shape humans into a particular mold. This is why it is important for human beings to keep the word of God upon their hearts. They must "teach them diligently" to their children and "shall talk of them when you sit in your house, and when you walk by the way, and when you lie down, and when you rise."[86] The contrasting of expressions like "sit at your house" and "walk along the way," and "lie down" and "rise" is called a merism. It explains the totality of a thing by contrasting extremes, like the biblical reference of "from Dan to Beersheba" represented the totality of Israel.[87] In other words, the truth of God's word should infuse and guide every action and decision and should be weighed against every philosophy.

In addition to holding up the biblical view of marriage and family as normative and educating children according to a biblical worldview, better mental stimulation is needed during the early years of childhood, especially

84. Louw and Nida, "Be Transformed. . .," 155.

85. Hiebert, "Presentation and Transformation," 319–23. This paragraph is largely based on Hiebert's exegesis of Romans 12:2.

86. Deuteronomy 6:6–7.

87. Gentry, "Raising Children," 100.

in homes of children of Americans of African descent. Apparently there is a short window, from birth to about three years old, where brain stimulation or the lack thereof can have lifelong consequences. Thus, if the child's brain is highly stimulated with games, sights, sounds, people reading to them, and the like, their brains will develop in such a way that will increase their intelligence for life. However, in atmospheres that lack positive stimulation or are toxic, intelligence is also affected, but negatively.[88] If Americans of African descent want their children to have every advantage, they need to start training their children from birth. As mentioned earlier, people from the higher socio-economic classes whose children do very well in school and later in adulthood do two things that give their children a necessary boost: they take special care for the development of their children from the time of conception and they make the intellectual stimulation of babies a priority.[89] Because this is such an urgent necessity, prenatal and childrearing classes should be encouraged for every American of African descent parent, and especially for those in lower socio-economic areas who may be ignorant of the research in this area.

A good start would be for well-to-do churches or groups of churches to found evangelistic-based Christian schools in communities of Americans of African descent that place special focus on those areas of educational development where the community lacks. Although this would be costly, it would pay off in the end. These schools would provide the opportunity for greater understanding of Christian principles and will result in higher graduation rates and lower incarceration rates. Since these schools would be free private facilities, they could require adult parenting classes that would be based on the individual needs of each family. As well, they could offer special incentives for later enrollment to those who take prenatal and childrearing classes before their babies are born. These schools could provide community services to offer support and spiritual guidance to young families and could serve as a beacon of evangelism in low income areas. Raphël Franck and Laurence R. Iannaccone found that there is a correlation between governmental educational spending and a decline in religiosity. Hence, schools are one of society's greatest tools for indoctrination, and it seems that the American secular educational system is helping to turn people away from God.[90] If churches are serious about making last-

88. Steinburg, *Age of Opportunity*, 9, 22.

89. Murray, *Coming Apart*, 39.

90. Franck and Iannaccone, "Religious Decline in the 20th Century West," 406.

ing disciples, they must make the investment now and counter the secular push for the minds of America's children.

Charles Murray pointed out that one of the main reasons that early Americans had a collective religious worldview is because children were socialized through schools. When immigrants came to America, American values were widely accepted by them within a relatively short period of time simply because American values were inculcated upon children through the educational system. However, by the middle of the twentieth century a variant value system began to arise that rejected the idea that American children should be indoctrinated with traditional American values; thus, the former underlining value-laden paradigm was exchanged for a secular one.[91] In earlier America, even those who were unchurched and nonreligious often accepted the Judeo-Christian worldview because they saw it as the best option for their families and society as a whole.[92] However, in contemporary society, many actually believe that the traditional Judeo-Christian ethic and worldview is harmful to society, likening Christians to bigots, homophobes, and sexists pigs.[93]

Many young people who were raised in a Christian setting begin to exchange their religion for secularism during adolescence, and the majority completely leave the church as young adults. Some return later, but many do not.[94] Lifeway Research estimates that 70 percent of young people leave church and only about 35 percent of those eventually return.[95] This means that almost two-thirds never return. Yet, by the time they return, many of them have to live the remainder of their lives in the wake of their mistakes.[96] These young people are not totally rejecting everything they learned as children but they are accepting alternative views of God and morality. In one survey, the most prevalent answer given of why they left their former faith is summed up as "intellectual skepticism."[97] One writer aptly described the belief system of these young people as "Moralistic Therapeutic Deism," because their existence is "a self-centered worldview, in

91. Murray, Coming Apart, 140–42.

92. Murray, Coming Apart, 200.

93. Dickerson, Great Evangelical Recession, 50, 53–55.

94. Mervwe, Grobler, Strasheim, and Orton, "Getting Young Adults Back to Church," 1.

95. "Church Dropouts." 4.

96. Dickerson, Great Evangelical Recession, 103.

97. McDowell and McDowell, Unshakable Truth, 24.

which personal happiness is the highest goal and a distant God is taken for granted in the background."[98] Once again, these young people have been bombarded with conflicting reports about how they should live and what they should value. Just like most human beings, young people tend to follow whatever is popular and have never really understood the foundations of faith. However, those young people who persevered in their faith did so because their faith had "personal relevance," or they saw how their faith had significance both now and in their future lives.[99] Simply put, the ones who stuck with their faith did so because they saw a reason to do so. They understood why faith is important. Having a unified worldview put forth by both the child's family and his or her school will greatly reduce the ambiguity and display relevance to young minds. One does not need to be a proverbial rocket scientist to see the correlation. The home and the school, working together, makes lasting foundations in a person's life because they best provide the basic philosophies through which a person lives. The fact that wherever there is an increase of governmental spending on secular education, there is also a decrease in religiosity shows that public education has a great effect on worldview.[100] Whatever social and philosophical structures that are intertwined with a person's family and primary education, though they be secular, religious, or other, will have the greatest influence on how that person will live and build his or her life.

America's secular society is winning the battle for America's soul. John S. Dickson reported that "Americans under the age of thirty-five are four times more likely to be atheistic, agnostic, or nonreligious."[101] Hence, he predicts that after the older generation passes away, the American cultural landscape will be radically transformed, and antagonism toward the Judeo-Christian worldview will increase.[102] The Barna Research group found that 65 percent of adults in America believe that standard morality should be determined by culture.[103] Barna further documented that "nearly half (45 percent) of non-religious adults perceive Christianity to be extremist."[104] Furthermore, in an August 2015 survey, 17 percent of Americans of African

98. Dickerson, *Great Evangelical Recession*, 105.

99. "Church Dropouts," 36.

100. Franck and Iannaccone, "Religious Decline in 20th Century West," 386.

101. Dickerson, *Great Evangelical Recession*, 46.

102. Dickerson, *Great Evangelical Recession*, 46.

103. "End of Absolutes."

104. "Five Ways Christianity is increasingly Viewed as Extremist."

descent said that they believed that churches contribute to racial problems while only 9 percent of whites thought so.[105]

If the church is serious about making a lasting effect, it must begin the reconstruction of human values at the foundational level when these philosophies are first formed. Parents must be trained to recognize which type of family unit works best, how to exercise proper discipline in a controlled and loving manner, and how to practice value formation through family relationships. As well, children must be taught how to respect authority, especially in the home. Their educational environment must be based on an understanding that all humans were created in the image of the one true God, and he has given the best instructions on how humans should live.

Having said the above, one must concede that most families do not fit the ideal. Considering that there are no perfect humans on Earth today, all families are deficient in one way or another. So what should be done, since there are no perfect families? Fortunately, the omniscient God who created humans in his image anticipated a broken world, and therefore there are other options. Alternative models for family value formation will be discussed in the following chapter. Although it must be emphasized that God's best is the ideal, and the ideal should always be the goal, one must do the best to live out God's will in the situations in which he or she finds himself or herself.

105. "Five Ways Christianity is increasingly Viewed as Extremist."

Chapter 5

Practical Helps

The Bible testifies that all humans are sinful before God. As was shown in chapter 3, sin is not a black or a white thing, it is a human thing. Psalm 14:2–3 says, "The Lord looks down from heaven on the children of man, to see if there are any who understand, who seek after God. They have all turned aside; together they have become corrupt; there is none who does good, not even one." Romans 3:9 testifies, "What then? Are we Jews any better off? No, not at all. For we have already charged that all, both Jews and Greeks, are under sin." Since this is true, one can rightly conclude that there are no perfect families. Although American of African descent families have been decimated to a greater extent than families of other racial groups, the same corruption, to some extent, is spreading through all human families.

Yet, given the fact that the perfect family does not exist in this world, one should not assume that any family model is as good as another. There is an ideal to which humans should attain. That ideal was given in Genesis 1 and 2. In essence, the ideal is for a husband and wife who are committed to one another in a one-flesh, lifelong relationship to beget and raise their biological children under the fear of God. However, along with sin often comes broken relationships, some of which are of little or no fault to one party. With all that being said, in order to attain to maximum human flourishing even in the midst of this sinful and rebellious world, it is expedient upon humans to conform, as much as possible, to that ideal given by God.

In this chapter, the idea of how imperfect family structures should attempt to conform to the biblical model will be discussed. When humans find themselves in family structures that do not conform to God's ideal, they can either choose to be powerless and remain victims or choose to be powerful by accepting where they are and taking positive steps to better their situation.[1] There are certain practices that the Bible affirms as acceptable and others that it rejects as unacceptable. Those practices that God deems as acceptable will work for the good of those who practice them.[2] All family models, as much as is possible, must seek the best principles of what is deemed acceptable before God to attain the best possible outcome for human flourishing.

The Bible and Family Values

In a 2005 paper, David L. Petersen argued that traditional family values touted by groups like Focus on the Family and the Family Research Council rarely have explicit biblical support. In surveying families in the book of Genesis, Peterson found that many of those chronicled do not reflect the one held high by family values advocates.[3] The values that Peterson found highlighted were threefold. The first was an "expansive view of the family" where the family was seen as more than the nuclear, but consisted of grandparents, uncles, aunts, as well as other extended family members and even slaves. The second value identified by Peterson was that a lax view of sexuality in marriage (like polygamy and the uses of concubines) supported the continuance of the family. In other words, slaves were often given to be concubines to present suitable heirs so the family would continue over generations. Peterson's third family value was that families resolved conflicts in ways that avoided violent behavior.[4] However, the Bible states what really happened, not what should have been or even what was best. The Bible records the actions of sinful humans—the good, the bad, and the ugly—in the midst of God working out his salvific plan. It is a mistake to assume that all the actions of godly biblical characters are exemplary for all humans today because they too were sinful.[5] Family values are formulated

1. Lee, *Power Principle*, 14.
2. Deuteronomy 10:13.
3. Petersen, "Genesis and Family Values," 5–6.
4. Peterson, "Genesis and Family Values," 15–22.
5. Stuart, *Old Testament Exegesis*, 181.

from those standards of marriage and family that correspond with God's original intention for humanity.[6] The heroes of the Bible were sinful human beings; they were not perfect.

In response to Peterson's question about the family values the Bible espouses, one cannot simply look to examples of sinful human beings reported in the Bible, but one should look to passages that state what God originally intended for human beings. When Jesus said in Matthew 5:48, "You must therefore be perfect, as your heavenly Father is perfect," he was not telling his listeners that he expected them to never sin again. He was setting a goal to pursue. The real fact that humans can never attain sinless perfection in this age is no excuse for them to remain preoccupied with and settle in failure.[7] Each person's goal should be to conform himself or herself as much as possible with God's ideal, even in the midst of this sinful environment. Only by doing this can a person have the greatest chance to attain to maximum human flourishing.[8] As stated earlier, Genesis 2:24–25 states the original intention of one man and one woman to be the foundation for the family, and Jesus supported this view in Mathew 19:3–9.

Alternative Provision for Family Support

Peterson is correct in an unintended consequence to his article: godly people have adapted to their less-than-perfect situations by attempting to stay in line with godly principles as much as they were aware and able. Since most, if not all, of the Scriptures that exist today had not been written during patriarchal times, it can be assumed that none of the patriarchs identified in Genesis had access to the corpus of Scripture as believers do today. Hence Peterson's first identified biblical family value, "defining family in expansive terms,"[9] is actually the biblical key to assist imperfect hu-

6. Dobson, *Complete Marriage and Family Guide*, 411.

7. Thomas, *Evangelical Hermeneutics*, 57.

8. Deuteronomy 10:12–13 says, "And now, Israel, what does the Lord your God require of you, but to fear the Lord your God, to walk in all his ways, to love him, to serve the Lord your God with all your heart and with all your soul, and to keep the commandments and statutes of the Lord, which I am commanding you today for your good?" The terms "fear," "walk in his ways," "serve," and "love" are covenantal terms and thus they are reciprocated with God's blessing. Hence, doing what is right before God will result in the doer's good. See Ajith Fernando, *Deuteronomy: Loving Obedience to a Loving God*, Preaching the Word, ed. R. Kent Hughes (Wheaton, IL: Crossway, 2012), 339–42.

9. Peterson, "Genesis and Family Values," 22.

man families. Families that lack the biological father, the biological mother, or anything else must supplement that absence with a substitute. Programs are not the answer, but loving and supportive relationships are.

The Hebrew family adapted in many ways to meet various practical needs. The term used for "family" in the Hebrew Bible is מִשְׁפָּחָה, and it can refer to the immediate household or extend to the clan. It is used 303 times in the Bible. The word goes beyond the nuclear family to the extended family or clan.[10] However, not only kinship but also servants and all who travelled with Abraham, including pets and beasts of burden, fell under his covenant protection and were part of his household.[11] As well, in an attempt to protect family property and keep family members out of poverty, Hebrew law supported levirate marriage, where a man could marry his brother's widow. In that union, the widow of the deceased brother would receive support, and the first male offspring would maintain the dead brother's name and inheritance.[12] Since most marriages were arranged, love was not the chief reason for the union; the conservation of the group was the main objective. However, just as in relationships of consanguinity, love often came later. Although polygamy was allowed under certain cultural circumstances, it was never officially sanctioned in the Bible; monogamy was considered the ideal. Hence, the Hebrew family's main function was the protection of the interests of the group. For example, if an individual fell into poverty and had to be sold into slavery, the nearest kin (i.e., kinsman redeemer) had the duty to support the welfare of the group by buying the person from slavery.[13]

In the New Testament, the family is still important but not as important as the larger family of God. Jesus seemed to elevate the bond shared between believers above the bond of consanguinity. Matthew 12:46–50 records an event where Jesus was told that his family sought to converse with him. Rather than go out to them, Jesus concluded in verses 49b and 50, "Here are my mother and brothers! For whoever does the will of my Father in heaven is my brother and sister and mother." On another occurrence recorded in Luke 11:27–28, a woman in the crowd blurted out "Blessed is the womb that bore you, and the breasts at which you nursed!" However, Jesus replied, "Blessed rather are those who hear the word of God and keep it." Furthermore although Mathew 13:55 and Mark 6:3 testify that Jesus

10. Zobel, "מִשְׁפָּחָה," 80.

11. See Exodus 20:10

12. See Deuteronomy 25:5–10.

13. C. J. H. Wright, "Family," 47–49.

had brothers, Jesus left his mother in the care of the beloved disciple in John 19:26–27. This was most likely done because his brothers were not yet believers.[14] In saying these things, Jesus was in no way diminishing the importance of the family.[15] Yet, he was pointing out that the ideology of worshipping the one true God and fidelity to him is of primary importance.[16] Charles H. Talbert concluded that Jesus taught that the family of believers replaced the natural family.[17] However, a better understanding of these verses would be that worship of God and spiritual relationships based on that worship takes priority over natural relationships rather than replaces them.[18]

Thus, when the care of family relations breaks down, a person's spiritual family should fill in the gaps. Children raised in Christian families should never be without models of authentic maleness and femaleness. If Americans of African descent, as well as other groups that are in trouble, are to be redirected, extended Christian families need to step in and fill the gaps. This is one of the reasons that Jesus said in John 13:35, "By this all people will know that you are my disciples, if you have love for one another." Those outside the covenant of faith should witness authentic, familial, Christian love between believers and recognize Christ's disciples, because they do what he did. Biblical love is less about what one feels, because Christians are commanded to "love your enemies."[19] It is quite difficult for a person to have a warm and fuzzy feeling for someone who wants him or her dead or injured in some way. The biblical love of God is more about what a person

---

14. Mounce, *Luke-Acts*, 635. See also John 7:5.

15. In Mark 7:9–13, Jesus rebuked the religious leaders for placing their tradition above God's stated word. Jesus quoted the fifth commandment, "Honor your father and mother" (Ex 20:12; Deut 5:16) and "whoever reviles father or mother must surely die" (Ex 21:17), in the context of parents receiving financial support from children. However, the religious leaders began a tradition that a person could dedicate to God whatever the parent would have received as help, and thus the parents would not receive the financial assistance required by Scripture. Jesus said that this tradition was in direct contradiction to God's word. Hence, Jesus did not advocate an abdication of duty to care for aging parents under the guise of spirituality. He did, however, place dedication to him as priority above all things. Paul said in 1 Timothy 5:8, "But if anyone does not provide for his relatives, and especially for members of his household, he has denied the faith and is worse than an unbeliever."

16. Sproul, *St. Andrew's Expositional Commentary Matthew*, 406.

17. Talbert, *Matthew*, 157.

18. Trites and Larkin, *Gospel of Luke, Acts*, 181.

19. Matthew 5:44.

does. Paul quoted Proverbs 25:21 in agreement with Jesus' command to love one's enemies by saying, "if your enemy is hungry, feed him; if he is thirsty, give him something to drink."[20] As well, the apostle John argues that talking love without practicing love is worthless. After first saying that humans know love by what Jesus did because "he laid down his life for us," in the same way, he concludes, "let us not love in word or talk but in deed and truth."[21] Hence, if Christians are to fulfil their duty in showing love to families in need, they must pick up the slack by being an extended family to single parents or those without role models of what authentic humanity, as bearers of the image of God, should be.

There is no wonder that the New Testament local congregation took on the form of house churches. From what is known, New Testament Christian congregations met exclusively in houses for the first 120 years or so. Some of those houses used for churches began to be adapted exclusively for Christian worship for the next one-hundred years after that. It was not until about AD 250 that church-type rectangular buildings began to be utilized in some places for public worship.[22] The early house churches remained small and intimate, simply because most houses could hold no more than fifteen to twenty people. When they grew beyond what the house could hold, they divided and began a new fellowship in another house.[23] Hence, these groups functioned much like a family unit. They cared for personal needs and held each person in the group accountable to Christian standards. When people were disowned by their families for becoming Christians, the church family served as a new family unit. For those whose families were Christian, the church family served as an extended family to support what was already there or what may be lacking.[24] Even when the number of disciples had multiplied into thousands and the whole church was only in one place, Jerusalem, they met together as a large group in a part of the temple complex, but then they divided into smaller groups, "breaking bread in their homes" so true discipleship could take place.[25]

---

20. Romans 12:20.

21. John 3:16, 18.

22. Linton, "House Church Meetings in the New Testament Era," 230.

23. Atkinson and Comiskey, "Lessons from the Early House Church for Today's Cell Groups," 78.

24. Atkinson and Comiskey, "Lessons from the Early House Church," 81.

25. Acts 2:46.

However, today's church is couched in what has been referred to as a postmodern culture, and the ideologies that are shaping the structural foundations of today's American church are the same ones that shaped this present generation.[26] Although the number of worshippers in all major denominations is shrinking, many of the larger churches, with their celebrity-type leadership, are growing mainly because of transfer growth from smaller congregations.[27] Unless these larger churches make small groups foundational within their ministry structure, most people attending can walk in and out without significant, personal interaction with any other person.

The postmodern mindset is based on a nihilistic outlook where life is judged by how it affects the person at the moment. Since metanarratives do not exist in the postmodern mind, the only reality that matters is the person's own existential experiences.[28] Their concepts of divinity and spiritual devotion are privatized rather than religious, or that which is institutionalized; hence, they define themselves as spiritual rather than religious. Therefore, although postmodern thinkers are still in search of meaning and meaningful relationships, they tend to settle for that which is momentarily therapeutic. This is the very reason why many of today's churches devalue ancient biblical truths in exchange for motivational spiritual healing-type messages.[29] Therapeutic messages are attractive to postmodern thinkers. Yet, the end result of this type of spirituality is dedication to self and the creation of a god in one's own image and likeness, eclectically chosen in consistency with what one feels their god ought to be, rather than the way the true God reveals himself in holy Scripture. If a god exists for many with the postmodern outlook, he exists to serve the person, rather than vice versa, and his ultimate goal is to make the person happy.[30] The modern preoccupation with buying and consuming goods may be an attempt to purchase meaning in the lives of these postmodern dwellers.[31] As David Wells said, "Luxury and plenty, entertainment and recreation, sex and drugs, become ways of creating surrogate meaning or momentary distraction, or

26. Wells, *Above All Earthly Powers*, 123.

27. Dickerson, *Great Evangelical Recession*, 23.

28. Wells, *Above All Earthly Powers*, 67–68, 74.

29. Wells, *Above All Earthly Powers*, 109–10, 115, 123.

30. Dickerson, *Great Evangelical Recession*, 105.

31. Wells, *Above All Earthly Powers*, 77.

at least some numbness."[32] Many of today's churches are designed to appeal to the postmodern mindset, rather than to confront them with their rebellion against God and get them connected to God and his worshipping community.[33]

The content of the messages between churches of the same denomination is often no different throughout the varying races. The largest difference between churches of the same denomination that are predominately attended by black worshippers and those attended by predominately white worshippers is that black services are usually more emotionally charged than white services. Churches that are predominately attended by Americans of African descent affirm the speaker's message with words like "amen" and "hallelujah" and engage in "spontaneous physical worship" more often than in churches where the worshippers are predominately white.[34]

Hence, since postmodern people desire to connect with something real in the midst of their seemingly meaningless existence,[35] it is incumbent upon God's people to invite them to take part in caring and responsible small worshipping groups within God's household. People will respond to the message of Christ when they are overwhelmed by the truth of God displayed in the context of worshippers practicing God's love. When people meet regularly in small home church groups with other people who lovingly and naturally respond to spiritual, physical, and emotional needs, they will be transformed by God's Spirit and will find the belonging for which the human heart longs. Humans were not made to be in seclusion. Even when the world was perfect and no sin existed, there was still one thing that God said was not good. In Genesis 2:18 God said, "It is not good that the man should be alone . . . " This is why the theme song to the sitcom *Cheers* struck such a chord when it came out in 1982. Everybody wants to experience a sense of belonging, and "Sometimes you want to go where everybody knows your name and they're always glad you came."[36]

32. Wells, *Above All Earthly Pow'ers*, 192–93.

33. Wells, *Above All Earthly Pow'ers*, 123.

34. Edwards, "Race, Religion, and Worship: Are Contemporary African-American Worship Practices Distinct?" 30–32, 41.

35. Wells, *Above All Earthly Pow'ers*, 131.

36. Pritnoy and Angelo, *Where Everybody Knows Your Name*.

The Method of Giving Help: Displaying Love

In contrast to the postmodern outlook, which is self-centered, Christians are directed to love one another. The expression "one another" is used in over fifty instances throughout the New Testament.[37] Many of these "one another" exhortations are directing believers to love, show care, or forgive fellow believers. In the Christian meaning of the term, to love is to show the same concern for another as one would show for himself or herself.[38] Paul went further to say in Romans 13:10, "Love does no wrong to a neighbor; therefore love is the fulfilling of the law." Hence, all the commandments are "summed up in this word: 'You shall love your neighbor as yourself.'"[39] Therefore, it is the Christian duty to show love to other Christians by caring for them by meeting real needs. As Jesus said, the way people will know his disciples is "if you have love for one another."[40]

The love of God through Christians can be seen through their care for the neediest in the first-century generation: widows and orphans. James, the Lord's earthly brother, said, "Religion that is pure and undefiled before God, the Father, is this: to visit orphans and widows in their affliction, and to keep oneself unstained from the world."[41] The Greek word for "visit," the present infinitive ἐπισκέπτεσθαι, can mean, "to care for," "to bring justice to," or "to go see a person with a helpful intent."[42] Amy L. Sherman suggests that the term "visit" means more in Scripture than just giving people what they need physically, but it actually has "the idea of imparting life."[43] This brings to mind what the Apostle Paul wrote to the Thessalonians. They were more than a ministry project, because he said, "So, being affectionately desirous of you, we were ready to share with you not only the gospel of God but also our own selves, because you had become very dear to us."[44] Hence,

---

37. Atkinson and Comiskey, "Lessons from the Early House Church," 81. See also Mark 9:50; John 13:14, 34, 35; 15:12, 17; Rom 12:10, 16; 13:8; 14:3, 19; 15:5, 7, 14; 16:16; 1 Cor 11:33; 16:20; 2 Cor 13:12; Gal 5:13, 26; 6:2; Eph 4:2, 25, 32; 5:19, 21; Phil 2:3; Col 3:9, 13, 16; 1 Thess 3:12; 4:9; 5:11, 13, 15; 2 Thess 1:3; Heb 3:13; 10:24, 25; Jas 4:11; 5:9, 16; 1 Pet 1:22; 4:8, 9, 10; 5:5, 14; 1 John 1:7; 3:11, 23; 4:7, 11, 12; 2 John 1:5.

38. Brower, *Mark*, 318.

39. Romans 13:9.

40. John 13:35.

41. James 1:27.

42. McCartney, *James*, 129.

43. Sherman, "Visiting Orphans and Widows," 26.

44. 2 Thessalonians 2:8.

the phrase "to visit . . . in their affliction" probably means more than writing a check or dropping off a meal or some clothes, it may carry the meaning of supporting them wholly, spiritually, physically, and psychologically, for the long haul through their time of difficulty. Christians are called to help make peoples' lives whole in areas where they are broken, and all humans, being sinful, are lacking somewhere. Since the word for visit is a present tense infinitive, it should be understood that it should be a Christian practice and lifestyle of visiting, not just an occasional or one-time event.

The one thing that those who were the neediest had in common in the first-century Roman world, the setting in which the New Testament was written, was their lack of family support to help meet basic needs.[45] In 1 Timothy 5, while talking about widows, Paul set a basic pattern. If there was a believer in the extended family who could meet the need, that person should meet it. However, if there were no believers available in the extended family who could meet the need, the church—as extended family—must step up and fill the void. In 1 Timothy 5:16, Paul said through the inspiration of the Spirit of the Lord, "If any believing woman has relatives who are widows, let her care for them. Let the church not be burdened, so that it may care for those who are really widows." Apparently, those who were "really widows" were those with no other option for support. Hence, those widows who had extended blood family members who were believers and could care for them should be supported by those family members.[46] In this way, the extended family of the church could focus on those with no other support.[47] As Paul said earlier in that same chapter, "But if anyone does not provide for his relatives, and especially for members of his household, he has denied the faith and is worse than an unbeliever."[48]

The twenty-first-century world is quite different than the first-century one, but the same biblical principles that the first-century church used to meet the needs of their fellow disciples should be extended through the

45. Sneed, "Israelite Concern for the Alien, Orphan, and Widow," 500.

46. Commentators often focus on the reason why the "believing woman" is pointed out as the one who should provide care for widows in verse 16. However, verse 4 of this same chapter and in the same context also says that "children" and "grandchildren" are "to show godliness to their own household and to make some return to their parents." Thus, although this type of care may have been considered the responsibility of women in first-century culture, the duty to make sure the care was provided fell on all children and grandchildren.

47. Towner, *Letters to Timothy and Titus*, 358–59.

48. 1 Timothy 5:8.

contemporary church. God is not calling his church in the twenty-first-century United States to mimic everything that was done in the first-century church. Ministry to the world must be incarnational. When Jesus came to Earth, he neither ceased to be who he was, nor did he cause humans to be culturally different from what they were, but he added humanity to his divinity and lived committed to God as a first-century Jewish Galilean man. However, he reinterpreted the already existing paradigms to be more consistent with how God created humans to be. The church must do the same in this twenty-first-century American culture in order to be incarnational as Jesus was incarnational. Those sinful and harmful paradigms and actions must be denounced, and gospel truths must be put in place to grow in the midst of twenty-first-century United States culture.[49] Hence, those who are considered needy will share certain similarities between the first and the twenty-first centuries, but there may also be vast differences culturally and in the way God's people are called to meet those needs.

Who are the "needy" in contemporary society today? Those designated as truly needy depend upon what is meant by needy. Are they needy economically, socially, spiritually, or physically? To some extent everybody is needy, "for all have sinned and fall short of the glory of God."[50] This is why every Christian needs to meet regularly with other Christians in worship and fellowship; they must give and receive encouragement to one another to keep on the proper path.[51] Mark A. Tatlock argues that James's referral to "widows and orphans" is seen by James's Jewish readers as "a kind of shorthand" in the Jewish Scriptures for all who are "poor."[52] The poor can be defined as those who are "utterly helpless, defenseless, in need of provision and protection."[53] Surely this definition can be extended in these contemporary times beyond the economically poor to those lacking resources in other areas. Jesus showed concern for every person with a need: lepers, the blind, prostitutes, and even the financially wealthy but morally corrupt and spiritually poor tax collectors.[54]

A major need in families of Americans of African descent is support to make up for family deficiencies; thus, many of them can be seen as poor

49. Barbour, "Seeking Justice and Shalom in the City," 304–05.
50. Romans 3:23.
51. Hebrews 10:25.
52. Tatlock, "Caring for the Needy," 284.
53. Tatlock, "Caring for the Needy," 278.
54. Tatlock, "Caring for the Needy," 282.

in familial support. Single mothers or fathers, fatherless or motherless children, people involved in unhealthy family situations, and people involved in toxic relationships can receive positive support from Christian brothers and sisters. Christian men can stand in for fatherless boys as surrogate uncles/mentors, and Christian women can stand in for girls who do not have positive role models as aunts/mentors. Christian married couples can model authentic loving relationships to make marriage attractive again to the younger generation, and Christian older married couples can mentor younger married couples. Older or more mature women can model authentic womanhood for younger women, and older or more mature men can model authentic manhood for young men. In small and intimate church house groups, Christian people can take an active interest in one another and add the family support that is often lacking in nuclear families. As well, those small Christian groups can get together to form a larger one and start Christian schools to support a Christian worldview for young, precious souls. Those who can, should add resources to areas of need where people lack. This involves more than just writing a check; it involves sharing one's life. Sometimes those costs, the ones that are priceless, are worth more than any material possession a person could share.

A widely used African proverb is, "It takes a village to raise a child." This refers back to a time when whole communities, in support of nuclear families, took part as aunts and uncles of children, because the whole community shared the same value system and trusted one another.[55] For Christians in today's secular world, this is not possible, because the secular world shares widely different values than Bible-believing Christians.[56] However, the worshipping community of the Christian should, although it often does not, fill this void as the village on whom people can rely. In order for a child to be raised in the way that God planned humans made in his image to be raised, the village must share the same worldview—a biblical worldview.

The Present Struggle

One of the major premises of this book is, if Americans of African descent are to ascend as a group, they have to stop seeing themselves as outsiders. They must understand that they, too, are Americans first. The ongoing struggle for civil rights has to be done with, and not against, other Americans.

55. Cara, "It Takes a Village to Raise a Child," 50.
56. Schaeffer, *Christian Manifesto*, 17–18.

Calling whites racist just because they are doing better as a group is not sufficient. Radical egalitarianism is not the answer for the black community; taking advantage of the equal opportunities is part of the answer. There is absolutely no legal impediment to any individual American from being anything that he or she aspires to be.

The modern liberal racial milieu is fighting a straw man. Before *Brown v. Board of Education* overturned the *Plessy v. Ferguson* decision in 1954, racial segregation was the law of the land. Even after that, states in the south rejected integration with Americans of African descent and would not allow them to eat at the same establishments, use the same water fountains, live in the same neighborhoods, be educated in the same schools, or have equal opportunity to employment as other Americans.[57] When Bobby Seale and Huey Newton founded the Black Panthers in 1966, they felt it was necessary for the protection of blacks against the massive prejudice and police brutality of the day. Police brutality was open, unabashed, and widespread in many southern states.[58] However, today, whatever examples that may be cited are isolated cases. Most police officers and agencies uphold the law.[59] As stated earlier, federal legislation, like the *Brown v. The Board of Education* in 1954, the Civil Rights Act of 1964, and the Voting Rights Act of 1965, has made any type of overt discrimination illegal in the United States.[60] In today's world, there is nothing prohibiting any citizen or group of citizens from becoming anything he, she, or they aspire to be. So why are Americans of African descent not doing as well as other racial groups in America?

The straw man being fought by many in the liberal wing of the black community is the myth that continual systemic racism is holding the community back. To hold the black community responsible for issues like "black-on-black crime" is seen by some as reinforcing "the racist premise that black pathology—not white supremacy—is chiefly responsible for the state's systematic assault on black people."[61] In other words, they are claiming that the United States, as a system, is upholding "white supremacy" and

---

57. Henretta and Brody, *America*, 816–17.

58. Nelson, "The *Longue Durée* of Black Lives Matter," 1735.

59. Meares, Tyler, and Gardener, "Lawful or Fair?," 298–300, 304, 308. Meares, et al., argues that police usually judge their own actions by whether the actions are lawful, while non-police usually judge police actions by police demeanor and how they are treated.

60. Henretta and Brody, *America*, 860.

61. Rickford, "Black Lives Matter," 36.

suppressing Americans of African descent through a "systematic assault on black people." They are not referring to the fifties, sixties, or seventies, but today, in a world where black faces are common in every major American structure, including the highest offices of the United States. The very fact that black faces are ubiquitous in every segment and social structure of society debunks the premise of some systematic assault by the country on black people.

One of the major arguments used to prove this systemic racism myth is the fact that, per capita, more Americans of African descent are incarcerated and negatively affected by police contacts than other races.[62] One writer compared blacks being shot by police in today's world with lynching in times past. According to that writer, police shooting black people and lynchings are both ways the establishment deters the progress of Americans of African descent and terrorizes the community into compliance. He further argued that "blacks are being killed by police at about the same rate as lynchings one hundred years ago."[63] Associating police action with lynching is inflammatory language, but is it a fair comparison? Can the mob violence of the unjustified lynchings during Jim Crow be compared to police action against blacks today?[64]

It is true that research shows that Americans of African descent are stopped and frisked more often than whites. However this, in itself, is not necessarily evidence of racism any more than the fact that since males are overwhelmingly stopped and frisked more often than females, that is evidence of gender bias.[65] In those areas that are considered high-crime, police tend to be more proactive in initiating police encounters in an attempt to maintain civility or to answer calls for service.[66] Those encounters, in turn, engender negative attitudes, by those encountered and their loved ones, toward police.[67] As well, it is empirically evidenced that communities that are more densely populated by blacks have higher levels of violent crime than other communities.[68] Hence, a major reason why Americans of Afri-

---

62. Larson, "Black Lives Matter and Bridge Building," 45.

63. Larson, "Black Lives Matter and Bridge Building," 48.

64. Henretta and Brody, *America*, 718–19.

65. Avdija, "Police Stop-and-Frisk Practices," 32.

66. Avdija, "Police Stop-and-Frisk Practices," 30.

67. Avdija and Giever, "Examining the Effect of Selected Demographic Characteristics on Crime-Reporting Behavior," 813.

68. Feldmeyer, Steffensmeier, and Ulmer, "Racial/Ethnic Composition and Violence,"

can descent are contacted by police and incarcerated more than whites and Hispanics is not necessarily because of prejudice, but because Americans of African descent, as a group, engage in criminal behavior more than whites and Hispanics.[69] Why is it this way for Americans of African descent? Hispanics suffer social and economic conditions quite similar to Americans of African descent, but their violent crime rates do not match those in predominately black communities. Are black folks inherently more violent than people of other races, or are there other factors at work here? Ben Feldmeyer, Darrel Steffensmeier and Jeffery T. Ulmer propose that "Latino populations are somewhat insulated or buffered from deleterious conditions that contribute to violence" because of the "protective influences of Latino immigrant communities—including strong kinship bonds, support networks, ethnic economies, and cultural bonds that enhance community social controls and provide a buffer against crime."[70] In other words, strong extended-family support units help to buffer Hispanics from the violent tendencies that have helped to devastate black communities.

There is no doubt; racism is alive and well in the United States and every other part of this world. As argued earlier, sin, violence, and racism is neither a white nor a black problem, it is a human problem, because all humans are sinful. Yet just because more blacks are stopped, frisked, and arrested in greater proportions, per capita, than whites and Hispanics, that cannot be automatically equated with racism. In a *Wall Street Journal* article, "The Myths of Black Lives Matter," Heather MacDonald reported that, over the last decade, 40 percent of police officers slain in the line of duty have been killed by Americans of African descent. Does this mean that Americans of African descent are prejudiced against police officers? As well, although Americans of African descent only comprise roughly 15 percent of the population of America's seventy-five largest counties, "blacks have been charged with 62% of all robberies, 57% of murders, and 45% of assaults" in those counties.[71] It is obvious that police contact with people committing crimes or those suspected of committing crimes is driving clashes between Americans of African descent and police. There is no proof that police are hunting down Americans of African descent and targeting them simply because of their race.

812.

69. Avdija, "Police Stop-and-Frisk Practices," 33–34.

70. Avdija, "Police Stop-and-Frisk Practices," 815–16.

71. MacDonald, "Myths of Black Lives Matter."

However, it must also be recognized that, although there are many race-baiters at work to help create the perception of racism between Americans of African descent and the American system, the fears felt by many must be respected. Since the message that the American system is racist and stacked against Americans of African descent seems to be the consensus of liberal academics and politicians, many accept it as part of their worldview. However, the facts speak for themselves. There is no reason to hold on to the message of victimology any longer. To equate the world today, though it may be imperfect, with the times of Jim Crow is a gross misrepresentation of the truth. The civil rights leaders of the 1960s would probably shudder today at the refusal of many Americans of African descent to take full advantage of the opportunities presented in modern America. These opportunities were the very ones for which they fought and died.

A Recap

As mentioned earlier, if Americans of African descent as a group are to better assimilate into society, they must reject the victim mentality that prevents them from attaining a higher social status, accept primary responsibility for their own successes or failures, and support value formation through the biblical concept of family. If Americans of African descent are to be more successful, they need not forget their distinctive heritage or their struggles, but they must do better at assimilating in the larger American culture. They can no longer see themselves as outsiders, but they, along with all who call themselves Americans, must adopt and maintain those good values that made America exceptional. Americans of African descent must reject degrading and destructive views of blackness,[72] and adopt those which are constructive, not only to their own race, but to all Americans. As the title "American of African descent" infers, they are Americans, just like all other racial groups who are citizens are Americans. They should not be seen, and neither should they see themselves, as second-class citizens. Hence, those distinctive qualities that make a person American, like the value of hard work, respect for lawful authority, faithful and strong marriages, and a value-governing faith, should also be accepted and shared by them.[73] The predominant culture should not be viewed by Americans of

72. Franklin, "Men's Studies, Men's Movement, and Study of Black Masculinities," 17.
73. Murray, *Coming Apart*, 130.

African descent as the exclusive possession of whites,[74] but those parts of American culture that make for success should be adapted as their own, regardless of their source. White people and the establishment should not be viewed as the enemy, but they should be viewed as partners, neither above or below Americans of African descent, and all Americans should work together to recover the good foundation on which this country was founded.

Americans of African descent have to stop seeing themselves as victims and take charge of their own future. Many are beginning with greater deficits in life than other racial and social groups, but with hard work they can overcome those issues as others have also overcome them. The claim of victimology is a claim of powerlessness.[75] It puts someone or something else in charge of another's destiny. As often said in this book, there is nothing inherent in American law or society that is keeping any citizen or group of citizens from being anything that he, she, or they legally desire to be. If any person or group is held back, it is due to other factors. All people are made in the image of God, therefore there is nothing inherent within any group that cannot be overcome with time and effort. If Americans of African descent are degraded in the perceptions of some, including themselves in some instances, those perceptions can be changed by giving evidence to the contrary.[76]

The answer to the issues faced by Americans of African descent cannot be found in programs.[77] Programs, at best, address the fruit of the issue rather than the root. The root issue that caused the problems is a worldview issue. It is a turning away from the God-ordained principles by which humans should live.[78] Thus, the only way to recover is to return to those principles by which God has ordained for humans to live. The major contributor to whether a child will be successful or will fail is the type of family in which the child is socialized. The traditional family unit lessens the likelihood of poverty, criminality, and promiscuity in children as well as increases educational standards, physical and mental health, and usually makes for better incomes when the children of those unions become

74. McWhorter, *Losing the Race*, 51.

75. Lee, *The Power Principle*, 19–21.

76. Williams, *Enough*, 125–27, 139–40.

77. Majors, "Conclusions and Recommendations," 305–06.

78. Bradley, *Black and Tired*, 23.

adults.[79] Therefore, the marriage unions between biological parents should be supported and held up as normative in communities of Americans of African descent. However, when some of those unions fail, as they will in this world of sin in which humans live, they need to be supported by Christian family members and the Christian fellowship of believers, as the extended family.

Isaiah 55:6–9 says, ""Seek the LORD while he may be found; call upon him while he is near; let the wicked forsake his way, and the unrighteous man his thoughts; let him return to the LORD, that he may have compassion on him, and to our God, for he will abundantly pardon. For my thoughts are not your thoughts, neither are your ways my ways, declares the LORD. For as the heavens are higher than the Earth, so are my ways higher than your ways, and my thoughts than your thoughts." It is not in the best interest of humans to seek answers to life's ultimate issues outside of God's plan. Since he is the creator of all that is, including humans, and he knows all, it is best to follow his instructions.

79. Schneider, Atteberry, and Owens, "Family Matters," 3, 10, 12, 14, 18, 22–25.

Bibliography

Aird, Enola. "Toward a Renaissance for the African-American Family: Confronting the Lie of Black Inferiority." *Emory Law Journal* 58 (2008) 7–21.

Anderson, Elijah. *Code of the Street; Decency, Violence, and the Moral Life*. New York: Norton, 1999.

Atkinson, Harley T. and Joel Comiskey. "Lessons from the Early House Church for Today's Cell Groups." *Christian Education Journal* 11 (2014) 75–87.

Aughinbaugh, Alison, Omar Robles, and Hugette Sun. "Marriage and Divorce: Patterns by Gender, Race, and Educational Attainment." United States Department of Labor Bureau of Labor Statistics (2013). http://www.bls.gov/opub/mlr/2013/article/ marriage-and-divorce-patterns-by-gender-race-and-educational-attainment.htm.

Avdija, Avdi S. "Police Stop-and-Frisk Practices: An Examination of Factors that Affect Officer's Decisions to Initiate a Stop-and-Frisk Police Procedure." *International Journal of Police Science and Management* 16 (2013) 26–35.

Avdija, Avdi S. and Dennis M. Giever. "Examining the Effect of Selected Demographic Characteristics on Crime-Reporting Behavior." *Journal of Alternative Perspectives in the Social Sciences* 4 (2012) 790–821.

Banks, Ralph Richard. *Is Marriage for White People? How the African American Marriage Decline Affects Everyone*. New York: Dutton, 2011.

Barbour, Claude Marie. "Seeking Justice and Shalom in the City." *International Review of Mission* 73 (1984) 303–09.

Bergmann, U. עֹז. In Vol. 2 of *Theological Lexicon of the Old Testament*. Edited by Ernst Jenni and Claus Westermann. Translated by Mark E. Biddle. Peabody, MA: Hendrickson, 1997.

Blomberg, Craig L. "Marriage, Divorce, Remarriage, and Celibacy: An Exegesis of Matthew 19:3–12." *Trinity* 11 (1990) 161–96.

Boateng II, Patrick. "Revealing True Electoral Patterns and What They Mean: A Conversation with Jamelle Bouie." *Harvard Journal of African American Public Policy* (2013) 63–66.

Bond, Michael. "The Secret of Success." *New Scientist* 221 (2014) 1–7.

Bork, Robert H. *Slouching Toward Gomorrah: Modern Liberalism and American Decline*. New York: Harper Perennial, 2003.

Bradley, Anthony B. *Black and Tired: Essays on Race, Politics, Culture, and International Development*. Eugene, OR: Wipf and Stock, 2011.

———, ed. *Keep Your Head Up: America's New Black Christian Leaders, Social Consciousness, and the Cosby Conversation*. Wheaton, IL: Crossway, 2012.

Bibliography

Briggs, Richard S. "Humans in the Image of God and Other Things Genesis Does Not Make Clear." *Journal of Theological Interpretation* 4 (2010) 111–26.

Brower, Kent. *Mark: A Commentary in the Wesleyan Tradition*. New Beacon Bible Commentary, edited by Alex Varughese, Roger Hahn, and George Lyons. Kansas City, MO: Beacon Hill, 2012.

Bush, Lawson V., and Edward C. Bush. "God Bless the Child Who Got His Own: Toward a Comprehensive Theory for African-American Boys and Men." *Western Journal of Black Studies* 37 (2013) 1–13.

Cara, Coral. "It Takes a Village to Raise a Child: Team Teaching and Learning Journeys." *The International Journal of Interdisciplinary Social Sciences* 6 (2012) 49–66.

Carter, Stephen L. "Religion, Education, and the Primacy of the Family." *Emory Law Journal* 58 (2008) 23–30.

"Chapter 3: Demographic and Economic Data, by Race." Pew Research Center (2013). http://www.pewsocialtrends.org/2013/08/22/chapter-3-demographic-economic-data-by-race/.

"Church Dropouts; How Many Leave Church Between Ages 18–22 and Why?" Lifeway Research (2007). http://lifewayresearch.com/wp-content/uploads/2014/01/Church-Dropouts_How-Many-Leave-Church-and-Why-8.07.2007.pdf.

Cloud, Henry and John Townsend. *Safe People*. Grand Rapids: Zondervan, 1995.

Cohn, D'vera, Jeffery S. Passel, Wendy Wang, and Gretchen Livingston. "Barely Half of U. S. Adults Are Married—A Record Low." Pew Research Center, Washington, DC (2011). http://www.pewsocialtrends.org/211/12/14/barely-half-of-u-s-adults-are-married-a-record-low/.

Cosby, William H., and Alvin F. Poussaint, *Come On People: On the Path from Victims to Victors*. Nashville: Thomas Nelson, 2007.

Craddock, Fed B. *Hebrews-Revelation*. Vol. 12. *The New Interpreter's Bible*, edited by Leander E. Keck and Fred Craddock. Nashville: Abingdon, 1998.

———. "The Letter to the Hebrews." In vol. 12 of *The New Interpreter's Bible: A Commentary in Twelve Volumes*, edited by Leander E. Keck, 1–173. Nashville: Abingdon, 1998.

Crenshaw, James L. "It's All About a Missing Rib: Human Sexuality in the Bible." *Perspectives in Religious Studies* 37 (2010) 267–82.

Crouch, Stanley. *The Artificial White Man: Essays on Authenticity*. New York: Perseus, 2004.

Daley, James, ed. *Great Speeches by Frederick Douglass*. Mineola, NY: Dover, 2013.

Dickerson, Debra. *The End of Blackness: Returning the Souls of Black Folk Back to Their Rightful Owners*. New York: Pantheon, 2004.

Dickerson, John S. *The Great Evangelical Recession: 6 Factors that Will Crash the American Church . . . And How to Prepare*. Grand Rapids: Baker, 2013.

Dickson, Patricia. "AARMS: The African American Relationships and Marriage Strengthening Curriculum for African American Relationships Courses and Programs." *Journal of African American Studies* 18 (2014) 337–52.

Dobson, James. *Bringing Up Boys*. Carol Stream, IL: Tyndale Momentum, 2001.

———. *Complete Marriage and Family Home Reference Guide*. Carol Stream, IL: Tyndale Momentum, 2000.

DuBois, W. E. B. *Morals and Manners among Negro Americans*. Atlanta: Atlanta University Press, 1914.

———. *The Souls of Black Folk*. New York: Penguin, 1982.

Bibliography

Dyson, Michael Eric. *Between God and Gangsta Rap*. Oxford: Oxford University Press, 1996.

———. *Is Bill Cosby Right? Or has the Black Middle Class Lost Its Mind?* New York: Basic Civitas, 2005.

———. *Know What I Mean? Reflections on Hip Hop*. New York: Basic Civitas, 2007.

Eberstadt, Mary. *How the West Really Lost God*. West Conshohocken, PA: Templeton, 2013.

Eddinger, Terry W. *Malachi: A Handbook of the Hebrew Text*. Waco, TX: Baylor University Press, 2012.

Edwards, Korie L. "Race, Religion, and Worship: Are Contemporary African-American Worship Practices Distinct?" *Journal for the Scientific Study of Religion* 48 (2009) 30–52.

Ellis, Carl, Jr. *Free At Last? The Gospel in the African-American Experience*. Downers Grove, IL: InterVarsity, 1996.

Elwang, William Wilson. "The Negroes of Columbia, Missouri: A Concrete Study of the Race Problem." MA diss., University of Missouri, 1904.

Feldmeyer, Ben, Darrell Steffensmeier, and Jeffery T. Ulmer. "Racial/Ethnic Composition and Violence: Size-of-Place Variations in Percent Black and Percent Latino Effects on Violence Rates." *Sociological Forum* 28 (2013) 811–41.

Fernando, Ajith. *Deuteronomy: Loving Obedience to a Loving God*, Preaching the Word, edited by R. Kent Hughes. Wheaton, IL: Crossway, 2012.

"Five Ways Christianity Is Increasingly Viewed as Extremist." *Barna Research* (2016). https:/www.barna.com/research/five-ways-christianity-is-increasingly-viewed-as-extremist/.

Fogle, Calvin D. "The Etymology, Evolution and Social Acceptability of 'Nigger,' 'Negro,' and 'Nigga.'" *Insights to a Changing World Journal* 2013 (2013) 82–125.

Fortunati, Leopoldina. "Media Between Power and Empowerment: Can We Resolve This Dilemma?" *Information Society* 30 (2014) 169–83.

Foster, Francis Smith. *'Til Death Do Us Part: Love and Marriage in African America*. Oxford: Oxford University Press, 2010.

Franck, Raphaël, and Laurence R. Iannaccone. "Religious Decline in the 20th Century West: Testing Alternative Explanations." *Public Choice* 159 (2014) 385–414.

Franklin III, Clyde W. "Ain't I a Man? The Efficacy of Black Masculinities for Men's Studies in the 1990s." In *The American Black Male*, ed. Richard G. Majors and Jacob U. Gordon, 271–83. Chicago: Nelson-Hall, 1994.

———. "Men's Studies, the Men's Movement, and the Study of Black Masculinities: Further Demystification of Masculinities in America." In *The American Black Male*, ed. Richard G. Majors and Jacob U. Gordon, 4–19. Chicago: Nelson-Hall, 1994.

Franklin, John Hope, and Alfred A. Moss, Jr. *From Slavery to Freedom: A History of Negro Americans*, 8th ed. Boston: McGraw-Hill, 2000.

Franklin, Robert M. *Crisis in the Village: Restoring Hope in African American Communities*. Minneapolis: Fortress, 2007.

Fretheim, Terence E., Walter Brueggemann, and Walter C. Kaiser. *Genesis-Leviticus*, edited by Walter Brueggemann and Walter C. Kaiser. Vol. 1. *The New Interpreter's Bible*. Nashville: Abingdon, 1994.

Gaylord-Harden, Noni K., Arie Zakaryan, Donte Bernard, and Sarah Pekoc. "Community-Level Victimization and Aggressive Behavior in African American Male Adolescents: A Profile Analysis." *Journal of Community Psychology* 43 (2015) 502–19.

Geisler, Norman. *Systematic Theology.* 4 vols. Minneapolis: Bethany House, 2004.

Gennetian, Lisa A. "One or Two Parents? Half or Step Siblings? The Effect of Family Structure on Young Children's Achievement." *Journal of Popular Economics* 18 (2005) 415–36.

Gentry, Peter J. "Sermon: Raising Children, the Christian Way." *The Journal of Discipleship and Family Ministry* 2 (2012) 96–108.

George, Nelson. *Hip Hop America.* New York: Penguin, 1998.

Gill, John. *An Exposition of the First Book of Moses Called Genesis.* Springfield, MO: Particular Baptist, 2010.

Gordon, Brian C., Mike A. Perko, Lori W. Turner, James D. Leeper, Stuart L. Usdan, and Samory T. Pruitt. "The Influence of Sexually-Oriented Music on Minority Adolescent's Sexual Initiation." *American Journal of Health Studies* 27 (2012) 214–26.

Grudem, Wayne. *Making Sense of Man and Sin: One of Seven Parts from Grudem's Systematic Theology.* Grand Rapids: Zondervan, 2011.

————. *Politics According to the Bible: A Comprehensive Resource for Understanding Modern Political Issues in Light of Scripture.* Grand Rapids: Zondervan, 2010.

Gutierrez, Ian A., Lucas J. Goodwin, Katherine Kirkinis, Jacqueline Mattis. "Religious Socialization in African American Families: The Relative Influence of Parents, Grandparents, and Siblings," *Journal of Family Psychology* 28 (2014) 779–89.

Harper, Kyle. "*Porneia*: The Making of a Christian Sexual Norm." *Journal of Biblical Literature* 131 (2011) 363–83.

Harris, Shanette M. "Black Male Masculinity and Same Sex Friendships." *Western Journal of Black Studies* 16 (1992) 74–81.

Hartley, John E. "Genesis." In vol. 1 of *New International Biblical Commentary,* edited by Robert L. Hubbard Jr. and Robert K. Johnson. Peabody, MA: Hendrickson, 2000.

Hattery, Angela J., and Earl Smith. "Families of Incarcerated African American Men: The Impact on Mothers and Children." *Journal of Pan African Studies* 7 (2014) 128–52.

Henretta, James A., and David Brody. *America: A Concise History.* Boston: Bedford/St. Martin's, 2010.

Herrnstein, Richard J. and Charles Murray. *The Bell Curve: Intelligence and Class Structure in American Life.* New York: Free Press, 1994.

Heth, William A. "Jesus on Divorce: How MY Mind Has Changed." *Southern Baptist Theological Seminary* 6 (2002) 4–29.

Hiebert, D. Edmond. "Presentation and Transformation: An Exposition of Romans 12:1–2." *Bibliotheca* 151 (1994) 309–24.

Hill, Andrew E. *Malachi.* New York: Doubleday, 1998.

Hoekema, Anthony A. *Created in God's Image.* Grand Rapids: Eerdmans, 1986.

Hood, Kristina, Joshua Brevard, Anh Bao Nguyen, and Fay Belgrave. "Stress Among African American Emerging Adults: The Role of Family and Cultural Factors." *Journal of Child and Family Studies* 22 (2013) 76–84.

Hooks, Bell. *We Real Cool: Black Men and Masculinity.* New York: Routledge, 2004.

Hopkins, Dwight N. "A New Black Heterosexual Male." *Black Theology in Britain: A Journal of Contextual Praxis* 8 (2002) 214–27.

Hopkins, Dwight N. *Being Human: Race, Culture, and Religion.* Minneapolis: Fortress, 2004.

Hunter, James Davidson. *To Change the World: The Irony, Tragedy, and Possibility of Christianity in the Late Modern World.* Oxford: Oxford University Press, 2010.

Bibliography

Hutchinson-Long, Betty J., "Paradigm Shift: Ministering to Youth in a Postmodern Age Using a Family-Based Model for Ministry in an African-American Church in Hampton, Virginia" DMin diss., Regent University, 2004.

"Inmate Race," Federal Bureau of Prisons. http://www.bop.gov/about/statistics/statistics_inmate_race.jsp.

Jackson, Cecile. "Introduction: Marriage, Gender Relations and Social Change," *Journal of Development Studies* 48 (2012) 1–9.

Jefferson, Thomas. "The Declaration of Independence." *Historic American Documents*, Lit2Go Edition, (1776). http://etc.usf.edu/lit2go/133/historic-american-documents/4957/the-declaration-of-independence/.

Jenni, E. דמה. In Vol. 1 of *Theological Lexicon of the Old Testament*, edited by Ernst Jenni and Claus Westermann. Translated by Mark E. Biddle. Peabody, MA: Hendrickson, 1997.

Jenson, Robert W. "Christ as Culture 1: Christ as Polity." *International Journal of Systematic Theology* 5 (2003) 232–29.

Jesus, Diego Santos Vieira. "Leks and Popozudas: How Hip-Hop Influences Black Subjectivities at the Carioca Funk." *Delaware Review of Latin American Studies* 14 (2013) 5.

Johnson, Elizabeth A. "The Incomprehensibility of God and the Image of God Male and Female." *Theological Studies* 45 (1984) 441–65.

Johnson, Luke Timothy. *Hebrews: A Commentary*. Louisville: Westminster John Knox, 2012.

Johnson, Thomas K. "Christ and Culture." *Evangelical Review of Theology* 35 (2011) 4–16.

June, Lee N. Ed., *The Black Family: Past, Present, and Future*. Grand Rapids: Zondervan, 1991.

Kay, Bruce. "'One Flesh' and Marriage." *Colloquium* 22 (1990) 46–57.

Keil, C. F. and F. Delitzsch, *The Pentateuch*. Volume 1 in *Commentary on the Old Testament*. Ten Volumes. Grand Rapids: Eerdmans, 1986.

Kelley, Robin D. G. *Race Rebels: Culture, Politics, and the Black Working Class*. New York: Free Press, 1994.

Kemper, Gary, Hallie Kemper, and Casey Luskin. *Discovering Intelligent Design: A Journey into the Scientific Evidence*. Seattle: Discovery Institute, 2013.

Kennedy, John F. *A Nation of Immigrants*. New York: Harper Perennial, 2008.

Kilner, John F. "Humanity in God's Image: Is the Image Really Damaged?" *Journal of the Evangelical Theological Society* 53 (2010) 601–17.

"King's Dream Remains an Elusive Goal; Many Americans See Racial Disparities." Pew Research Center, Washington, DC (2013). http://www.pewsocialtrends.org/2013/08/22/kings-dream-remains-an-elusive-goal-many-americans-see-racial-disparities/.

Kistemaker, Simon J. *Acts*. New Testament Commentary. Edited by William Hendriksen and Simon J. Kistemaker. Grand Rapids: Baker Academic, 2001.

———. *Revelation*. New Testament Commentary, edited by William Hendriksen and Simon J. Kistemaker. Grand Rapids: Baker, 2001.

Kynes, William L. "The Marriage Debate: A Public Theology of Marriage." *Trinity Journal* 28 (2007) 187–203.

Larson, Eric D. "Black Lives Matter and Bridge Building: Labor Education for a 'New Jim Crow' Era." *Labor Studies Journal* 4 (2016) 37–66.

Lee, Blaine. *The Power Principle: Influence with Honor*. New York: Fireside, 1998.

Bibliography

Lee, Patrick, and Robert P. George. "What Male-Female Complementarity Makes Possible: Marriage as a Two-in-One-Flesh Union." *Theological Studies* 69 (2008) 641–62.

Lefkovitz, Alison. "Men in the House: Race, Welfare, and the Regulation of Men's Sexuality in the United States, 1961–1972." *Journal of the History of Sexuality* 20 (2011) 594–614.

Lewis, C. S. *Mere Christianity*. San Francisco: HarperSanFrancisco, 1952.

Lincoln, C. Eric. *The Black Muslims in America*. Grand Rapids: Eerdmans, 1994.

Linton, Gregory. "House Church Meetings in the New Testament Era." *Stone-Campbell Journal* 8 (2005) 229–44.

Liu, Shirley H. and Frank Heiland. "Should We Get Married? The Effect of Parents' Marriage on Out-of-Wedlock Children." *Economic Inquiry* 50 (2012) 17–38.

Livingston, Gretchen, and Kim Parker. "Chapter 1: Living Arrangements and Father Involvement." Pew Research Center, Washington, DC (2011). http://www.pewsocialtrends.org/2011/06/15/chapter-1-living-arrangemtns-and-father-involvement/.

Louw, J. P. and Eugene Albert Nida, ed. "Be Transformed . . . ," "μεταμορφοῦσθαι." In *Greek-English Lexicon of the New Testament: Based on Semitic Domains*. New York: United Bible Society, 1988, 89.

———, ed. "Do Not Be Conformed . . . ," "συσχηματίζεσθαι." In *Greek-English Lexicon of the New Testament: Based on Semitic Domains*. New York: United Bible Society, 1988, 89.

Lowry, Noelle Z. "The Image of God in Humanity: Fleshing Out the Bare Bones of Marital Oneness." *Priscilla Papers* 26 (2012) 13–15.

Mac Donald, Heather. "The Myths of Black Lives Matter." *The Wall Street Journal*, 9 July 2016. http://www.wsj.com/articles/the-myths-of-black-lives-matter-1468087453.

MacPherson, William. "The Stephen Lawrence Inquiry." Secretary of State for the Home Department (1999): 6.5, 6.7. https://www.gov.uk/government/uploads/system/uploads/attachment_data/file/277111/4262.pdf.

Majors, Richard. "Conclusion and Recommendations: A Reason for Hope – An Overview of the New Black Male Movement in the United States." In *The American Black Male*, ed. Richard G. Majors and Jacob U. Gordon, 299–315. Chicago: Nelson-Hall, 1994.

Markon, Kristian E., Robert F. Krueger, Thomas J. Bouchard Jr., and Irving J. Gottesman. "Normal and Abnormal Personality Traits: Evidence of Genetic Environmental Relationships in Minnesota Study of Twins Reared Apart." *Journal of Personality* 70 (2002) 661–94.

Marks, Loren, Katrina Tanner, Olena Nesteruk, Cassandra Chaney, and Jennifer Baumgartner. "A Qualitative Exploration of Why Faith Matters in African American Marriages and Families." *Journal of Comparative Family Studies* 43 (2012) 695–714.

Marshall, Jill E. "Community Is a Body: Sex, Marriage, and Metaphor in 1 Corinthians 6:12–7:7 and Ephesians 5:21–33." *Journal of Biblical Literature* 134 (2015) 833–47.

Matteson, Lindsay K., Matt McGue, and William G. Iacono. "Shared Environmental Influences on Personality: A Combined Twin and Adoption Approach." *Behavior Genetics* 43 (2013) 491–504.

McBride, Dominica. "Uplifting the Family: African American Parents' Ideas of How to Integrate Religion into Family Health Programming." *Journal of Child and Family Studies* 22 (2013) 161–73.

McCartney, Dan G. *James*. Baker Exegetical Commentary on the New Testament. Edited by Robert W. Yarbrough and Robert H. Stein. Grand Rapids: Baker Academic, 2009.

Bibliography

McDowell, Josh, and Sean McDowell. *The Unshakable Truth: How You Can Experience the 12 Essentials of a Relevant Faith.* Eugene, OR: Harvest House, 2010.

McIlhaney, Joe S. Jr., and Freda McKissic Bush. *Girls Uncovered: New Research on What America's Sexual Culture Does to Young Women.* Chicago: Northfield, 2011.

McNamee, Catherine B., and R. Kelly Raley. "A Note on Race, Ethnicity, and Nativity Differentials in Remarriage in the United States." *Demographic Research* 24 (2011) 293–312.

McWhorter, John. *Losing the Race: Self-Sabotage in Black America.* New York: Harper Perennial, 2001.

———. *Winning the Race: Beyond the Crisis in Black America.* New York: Gotham, 2006.

Meares, Tracey L., Tom R. Tyler, and Jacob Gardener. "Lawful or Fair? How Cops and Laypeople Perceive Good Policing." *The Journal of Criminal Law and Criminology* 105 (2016) 297–343.

Mincey, Krista D., Moya Alfonso, Amy Hackney, and John Luque. "Being a Black Man: Development of the Masculinity Inventory Scale (MIS) for Black Men." *Journal of Men's Studies* 22 (2014) 167–79.

Moore III, James L., Donna Y Ford, and H. Richard Milner. "Underachievement among Gifted Students of Color: Implications of Educators." *Theory into Practice* 44 (2005) 167–77.

Morris, Leon. *Hebrews-Revelation.* Vol. 12. *The Expositor's Bible Commentary*, edited by Frank E. Gaebelein and J. D. Douglass, 1–158. Grand Rapids: Zondervan, 1981.

Mounce, Robert H. *Luke-Acts.* Vol. 10. *The Expositor's Bible Commentary*, edited by Tremper Longman III and David E. Garland, 257–661. Grand Rapids: Zondervan, 2007.

Moynihan, Daniel Patrick. *The Negro Family: The Case for National Action.* By the Office of Policy Planning and Research, United States Department of Labor. Washington, DC: U. S. Government Printing Office, March 1965.

Murray, Charles. *Coming Apart: The State of White America, 1960–2010.* New York: Crown Forum, 2012.

Nelson, Alondra. "The *Longue Durée* of Black Lives Matter." *American Journal of Public Health* 106 (2016) 1734–37.

Nietzsche, Friedrich. *In the Genealogy of Morals.* Translated by Walter Kaufmann and R. J. Hollingdale. New York: Vintage, 1967.

Nyawalo, Mich. "From 'Badman' to 'Gangsta'": Double Consciousness and Authenticity, from African-American Folklore to Hip Hop." *Popular Music and Society* 36 (2013) 460–75.

Parks, Gregory S., and Shayne E. Jones. "'Nigger': A Critical Race Realist Analysis of the N-Word within Hate Crimes Law." *The Journal of Criminal Law and Criminology* 98 (2008) 1305–52.

Patrick, LeBrian A. "Outside Insiders: Remember the Time." *Journal of Pan African Studies* 7 (2014) 106–27.

"Quick Facts United States." United States Census Bureau. https://www.census.gov/quickfacts/table/PST045216/00.

Patterson, Orlando. *The Ordeal of Integration: Progress and Resentment in America's "Racial" Crisis.* Washington: Civitas/Counterpoint, 1997.

Patterson, Paige. *Revelation.* Vol. 39. *The New American Commentary*, edited by E. Ray Clendenen. Nashville: B & H, 2012.

Bibliography

Pearcey, Nancy. *Total Truth: Liberating Christianity from Its Cultural Captivity*. Wheaton, IL: Crossway, 2004.

Penny, John. "The Role of Family Relationships, Broken Homes, Gender, and Extended Families on African American Delinquency in an Urban Setting." PhD diss., Union Institute Graduate College, 2001.

Petersen, David L. "Genesis and Family Values." *Journal of Biblical Literature* 124 (2005) 5–23.

Peterson, Abby. "Who 'Owns' the Streets? Ritual Performances of Respect and Authority in Interactions Between Young Men and Police Officers." *Journal of Scandinavian Studies in Criminology and Crime Prevention* 9 (2008) 97–118.

Reiss, Moshe. "Adam: Created in the Image and Likeness of God." *Jewish Bible Quarterly* 39 (2011) 181–86.

Revell, Maria and Melanie N. Mcghee. "Evolution of the African American Family." *International Journal of Childbirth Education* 27 (2012) 44–48.

Richardson, Joseph B., Jr., Mischelle Van Brakle, and Christopher St. Vil. "Taking Boys Out of the Hood: Exile as a Parenting Strategy for African American Male Youth." *New Directions for Child and Adolescent Development* 2014 (2014) 11–31.

Rickford, Russell. "Black Lives Matter: Toward a Modern Practice of Mass Struggle." *New Labor Forum* 25 (2016) 34–42.

Robotham, Rosemarie. "The State of the Black American Family Survey." *Ebony* 69 (2014) 122–27.

Rose, Tricia. *Black Noise: Rap Music and Black Culture in Contemporary America*. Middletown, CT: Wesleyan University Press, 1994.

Sailhamer, John H. *Genesis-Leviticus*. Vol. 1. *The Expositor's Bible Commentary*, edited by Tremper Longman III and David E. Garland. Grand Rapids: Zondervan, 2008.

Sands, Paul. "The *Imago Dei* as Vocation." *Evangelical Quarterly* 82 (2010) 28–41.

Saucier, P. Khalil, and Tryon P. Woods. "Hip Hop Studies in Black." *Journal of Popular Music Studies* 26 (2014) 268–94.

Schaeffer, Francis A. *A Christina Manifesto*. Wheaton, IL: Crossway, 1981.

Schrock, David. "Equipping the Generations: Children: A Blessed Necessity for Christian Marriages." *Journal of Discipleship and Family Ministry* 4 (2013) 62–64.

Schneider, Barbara, Allison Atteberry, and Ann Owens. "Family Matters: Family Structure and Child Outcomes." *Alabama Policy Institute* (June 2005) 1–42. https://www.acpeds.org/wordpress/wp-content/uploads/FamilyMatters.pdf.

Segura-April, Desiree L. "Religion and the Family." In *Handbook of Religion: A Christian Engagement with Traditions, Teachings, and Practices*, ed. Terry C. Muck, Harold A. Netland, and Gerald R. McDermott, 781–89. Grand Rapids: Baker Academic, 2014.

Sherman, Amy L. "Visiting Orphans and Widows." *Family and Community Ministries* (2008) 26.

Sherlock, Charles. *The Doctrine of Humanity*. Downers Grove, IL: InterVarsity, 1996.

Sims, Cherie M. Collins. "Towards a 'New Way of Thinking' about African American Family Life in Urban Neighborhoods." PhD diss., University of Minnesota, 2013.

Smiley, Tavis. *How to Make Black America Better: Leading African Americans Speak Out*. New York: Anchor, 2002.

Sneed, Mark. "Israelite Concern for the Alien, Orphan, and Widow: Altruism or Ideology?" *Zeitschrift für diealttestamentliche Wissenchaft* 3 (1999) 498–507.

Sowell, Thomas. *Intellectuals and Race*. New York: Basic, 2013.

Bibliography

Spencer, F. Scott. "Scripture, Hermeneutics, and Matthew's Jesus." *Interpretation* 64 (2010) 368–78.

Spencer, William David. "Marriage and Singleness as Teaching Tools of the Image of God." *Priscilla Papers* 23 (2009) 5–7.

Sproul, R. C. *Lifeviews: Make a Christian Impact on Culture and Society*. Grand Rapids: Revell, 2006.

———. *St. Andrew's Expositional Commentary Matthew*. Wheaton, IL: Crossway, 2013.

Staples, Robert. *The Black Family: Essays and Studies*, 6th ed. Albany, NY: Wadsworth, 1999.

Steele, Shelby. *A Dream Deferred: The Second Betrayal of Black Freedom in America*. New York: Harper Collins, 1998.

Steenwyk, Sherry A. M., David C. Atkins, Jamie D. Bedics, and Bernard E. Whitley Jr. "Images of God as They Relate to Life Satisfaction and Hopelessness." *International Journal for Psychology of Religion* 20 (2010) 85–95.

Steinberg, Laurence. *Age of Opportunity: Lessons from the New Science of Adolescence*. Boston: Houghton Mifflin Harcourt, 2014.

Stuart, Douglas. *Old Testament Exegesis: A Handbook for Students and Pastors*, 4th ed. Louisville: Westminster John Knox, 2009.

Talbert, Charles H. *Matthew*. Paideia Commentaries on the New Testament, edited by Mikeal C. Parsons and Charles H. Talbert. Grand Rapids: Baker Academic, 2010.

Tatlock, Mark A. "Caring for the Needy: How Ministry to the Poor Reflects the Gospel." *The Master's Seminary Journal* 22 (2011) 271–87.

Taylor, Ronald D. "Kin Social Undermining, Adjustment and Family Relations Among Low-Income African American Mothers and Adolescents: Moderating Effects on Kin Social Support." *Journal of Child and Family Studies* 24 (2015) 1271–84.

Taylor, Ronald D., Mia Budescu, Azeb Gebre, and Irma Hodzic. "Family Financial Pressure and Maternal and Adolescent Socioemotional Adjustment: Moderating Effects of Kin Social Support in Low Income African American Families." *Journal of Child and Family Studies* 23 (2014) 242–54.

"The End of Absolutes: America's New Moral Code." *Barna Research* (2016). https://www.barna.com/research/the-end-of-absolutes-americas-new-moral-code/.

Thomas, Robert L. *Evangelical Hermeneutics: The New Versus the Old*. Grand Rapids: Kregel, 2002.

Towner, Philip H. *The Letters to Timothy and Titus*. The New International Commentary on the New Testament, edited by New B. Stonehouse, F. F. Bruce, and Gordon D. Fee. Grand Rapids: Eerdmans, 2006.

Towner, W. Sibley. "Clones of God: Genesis 1:26–28 and the Image of God in the Hebrew Bible." *Interpretation* 59 (2005) 341–56.

Trites, Allison A. and William J. Larkin. *Luke-Acts*. Vol. 12. *Cornerstone Biblical Commentary*, edited by Philip W. Comfort, 1–347. Carol Stream, IL: Tyndale House, 2006.

Vainio, Olli-Pekka. "*Imago Dei* and Human Rationality." *Zygon: Journal of Religion and Science* 49 (2014) 121–34.

Van der Mervwe, Michelle C., Anské F. Grobler, Arien Strasheim, and Lizré Orton. "Getting Young Adults Back to Church: A Marketing Approach." *Hervomde Teologiese* 69 (2013) 1–12.

VanGemeren, Willem A. *Psalms*. Vol. 5 *The Expositor's Bible* Commentary, edited by Temper Longman III and David E. Garland. Grand Rapids: Zondervan, 2008.

Bibliography

Visala, Aku. "*Imago Dei*, Dualism, and Evolution: A Philosophical Defense of the Structural Image of God." *Journal of Religion and Science* 49 (2014) 101–20.

Wagner, Peter. "United States Incarceration Rates by Sex, 2010." *Prison Policy Initiative*, 2010. https://www.prisonpolicy.org/graphs/genderic.html.

Warren, Kiesha. "Family Structure and Attachment and Their Role in Reducing Delinquency in the African American Family." PhD diss., Western Michigan University, 2002.

Washington, Booker T. *Up From Slavery*. New York: Penguin, 1986.

Wells, David F. *Above All Earthly Powers: Christ in a Postmodern World*. Grand Rapids: Eerdmans, 2005.

Wenham, Gordon J. *Genesis 1–15*. Word Biblical Commentary, vol. 1. Waco, TX: Word, 1987.

West, Cornel. *Hope on a Tightrope: Words and Wisdom*. Carlsbad, CA: Hay House, 2008.

———. *Race Matters*. Boston: Beacon, 1993.

Western, Bruce, and Christopher Wildeman. "The Black Family and Mass Incarceration." *The Annals of the American Academy of Political and Social Science* 621 (2009) 221–242. http://ann.sagepub.com/.

White, W. Jr. "Family." In *The Zondervan Encyclopedia of the Bible*, edited by Merrill Tenney. Grand Rapids: Zondervan. 2009.

Wildberger, H. צלם. In *Theological Lexicon of the Old Testament*, edited by Ernst Jenni and Claus Westermann. Translated by Mark E. Biddle. Peabody, MA: Hendrickson, 1997.

Wilkins, Erica J., Jason B. Whiting, Marlene F. Watson, Jody M. Russon, and Allena M. Moncrief. "Residual Effects of Slavery: What Clinicians Need to Know." *Contemporary Family Therapy* 35 (2013) 14–28.

Williams, Joseph M. and Julia Bryan. "Overcoming Adversity: High-Achieving African American Youth's Perspectives on Educational Resilience." *Journal of Counseling and Development* 91 (2013) 291–300.

Williams, Juan. *Enough: The Phony Leaders, Dead-End Movements, and Culture of Failure That Are Undermining Black America—and What We Can Do About It*. New York: Crown, 2006.

Willie, Charles Vert. *A New Look at Black Families*, 3rd ed. Dix Hills, NY: General Hall, 1988.

Wilson, Walter T. "Sin as Sex and Sex with Sin: The Anthropology of James 1:12–15." *Harvard Theological Review* 95 (2002) 147–68.

Wilson, William J. *When Work Disappears: The World of the New Urban Poor*. New York: Vintage, 1996.

Witte, John, Jr. "Why Two in One Flesh? The Western Case for Monogamy Over Polygamy." *Emory Law Journal* 64 (2015) 1675–1746.

Wright, C. J. H. "Family." In *The Anchor Bible Dictionary*, edited by David Noel Freedman. New York: Doubleday, 1992.

X, Malcolm and Alex Haley. *The Autobiography of Malcolm X*. New York: Ballantine, 1965.

Zerner, R. "The Holocaust." In *Evangelical Dictionary of Theology*, edited by Walter A. Elwell. Grand Rapids: Baker, 1984.

Zobel, Greifswald. "מִשְׁפָּחָה." In vol. 9 of *The Theological Dictionary of the Old Testament*, edited by G. Johannes Botterweck, Helmer Ringgner, and Heinz-Josef Fabry. Translated by David E. Green. Grand Rapids: Eerdmans, 1998.

Zuckerman, Diana, and Sarah Pedersen. "Child Abuse and Father Figures: Which Kind of Families are Safest to Grow Up In?" *National Center for Health Research* (2015).

Bibliography

http://center4research.org/violence-risky-behavior/violence-and-threats-in-the-home/father-figures-are-the-answer-but-whats-the-question/.

Made in the USA
San Bernardino, CA
22 May 2019